REINHOLD NIEBUHR

Reinhold Niebuhr

ON POLITICS, RELIGION, AND CHRISTIAN FAITH

Richard Crouter

OXFORD
UNIVERSITY PRESS

2010

OXFORD
UNIVERSITY PRESS

Oxford University Press, Inc., publishes works that further
Oxford University's objective of excellence
in research, scholarship, and education.

Oxford New York
Auckland Cape Town Dar es Salaam Hong Kong Karachi
Kuala Lumpur Madrid Melbourne Mexico City Nairobi
New Delhi Shanghai Taipei Toronto

With offices in
Argentina Austria Brazil Chile Czech Republic France Greece
Guatemala Hungary Italy Japan Poland Portugal Singapore
South Korea Switzerland Thailand Turkey Ukraine Vietnam

Published by Oxford University Press, Inc.
198 Madison Avenue, New York, New York 10016

www.oup.com

Library of Congress Cataloging-in-Publication Data
Crouter, Richard.
Reinhold Niebuhr on politics, religion, and Christian faith / by Richard Crouter.
p. cm.
Includes index.
ISBN 978-0-19-537967-9; 978-0-19-537968-6 (pbk.) 1. Niebuhr, Reinhold,
1892–1971. 2. Christianity and politics—History of doctrines—20th
century. I. Title.
BX4827.N5C76 2010
230.092–dc22 2009032668

Printed in the United States of America
on acid-free paper

ACKNOWLEDGMENTS

Reinhold Niebuhr had officially retired by the time I arrived to study at New York's Union Theological Seminary in the 1960s. His works were a mainstay of the seminary classroom; his presence was deeply felt in the life of the institution. Although I was not his student, my wife, Barbara, and I made a point of hearing him on the occasions when he spoke or preached. My work as a historian of theology took me to earlier periods of Christianity, first to the ancient church and then to nineteenth-century German Protestantism, where I specialized in the thought of Friedrich Schleiermacher (1768–1834), the premier theologian of modern theological liberalism. Looking back now after years of teaching in the Department of Religion at Carleton College in Northfield, Minnesota, I see how Niebuhr's approach to theology has shaped my thinking, even when I was not fully aware of it.

Working on this book has provided new challenges as well as large debts that I owe to others. Apart from touching on Niebuhr in classroom lectures and in an occasional op-ed piece, I first wrote about him when my Munich colleague and co-editor of *The Journal for the History of Modern Theology / Zeitschrift für Neuere Theologiegeschichte,* Friedrich Wilhelm Graf, invited me to contribute a chapter on Reinhold and H. Richard Niebuhr for a three-volume anthology that he edited (*Klassiker der Theologie*, Munich: C. H. Beck, 2005). The Reverend Professor Mark Chapman invited me to give the Jaspers Lecture in November 2005 at Ripon College Cuddesdon,

Oxfordshire, on the topic "Needing the Niebuhrs: The Plight of Protestant Theology in America." The Theological College at Cuddesdon, led by its principal, the Reverend Canon Professor Martyn Percy, offered a congenial setting in which to explore Niebuhr's teaching in the company of British students. Librarians in the Manuscript Division of the Library of Congress assisted in working with the Reinhold Niebuhr Papers during a research visit in early winter 2006.

Invitations to try out these ideas in teaching situations were graciously extended by Herb Fry at the First United Church of Christ, Northfield, Minnesota, in October 2006 and by the Reverend Gayle Marsh at All Saints Episcopal Church, also in Northfield, in March 2007. Paul R. Strickland, Executive Director of the Center for Religious Inquiry at St. Mark's Episcopal Cathedral in Minneapolis, kindly arranged for a minicourse on Niebuhr in March and April 2008. A lively exchange of views with the participants in these settings helped shape the questions and direction of this book.

From the outset, my editor at Oxford University Press, Cynthia Read, has shown keen interest in the project as well as patience in guiding it to completion. To her, and to outside readers for Oxford, I owe much gratitude.

Longtime colleagues at Carleton College helped to nurture this project, sometimes unawares. Special gratitude is owed to the late Robert W. Wood, teacher of Niebuhrian social ethics at Doshisha University, Japan, and then at Carleton College, who unfailingly shed light on the foibles of the human condition. Chaplain emeritus David Maitland, teaching assistant to Niebuhr in the 1950s at Union Theological Seminary, remains a valued source of Niebuhr memorabilia. Political theorist Michael P. Zuckert, now at Notre Dame, has always stood ready to engage in spirited discussion of Niebuhr. Perry C. Mason, who brings a philosopher's lens to such matters, has been a splendid conversation partner. In addition, I am grateful to Carleton College president Robert Oden and dean of the college Scott Bierman (now president of Beloit College) for supporting my work as an emeritus member of the faculty.

Various persons read and commented on the book's manuscript or on parts of it in the making. The list includes Reinhold Niebuhr's daughter, Elisabeth Sifton, and Marion Pauck, friend of the Niebuhrs and biographer of Paul Tillich with her late husband Wilhelm Pauck. Specialists in Niebuhr's Christian social ethics, Robin Lovin, Edmund Santurri, and Ronald Stone, generously offered wise counsel, as did Larry Rasmussen on an early draft of these ideas. Carleton and St. Olaf colleagues Lori Pearson, Robert Bonner, Perry C. Mason, Judith Mason, Julie Klassen, and Gordon Marino provided useful criticism, comments, and suggestions. My profound thanks go to all of these readers. The book is a stronger for having passed under their eyes, even if none of them are responsible for the final choices that I have made.

In addition to thanking these careful readers, I am grateful to other colleagues and friends for their ongoing interest in my work, including the present Niebuhr project. Among others, this list includes Ted Vial, Julia Lamm, Brent Sockness, Walter Wyman, Jr., Dawn DeVries, Paul Capetz, David Possen, Ian Barbour, Bardwell L. Smith, Anne E. Patrick, Louis Newman, Roger Jackson, Michael McNally, Asuka Sango, Aimee Chor, Harry Williams, Mary Wood, Thomas Clough, Jewelnel Davis, the late Frank Reilly, Bill Hunt, Daniel Swenson, Friedrich Wilhelm Graf, Alf Christophersen, and Charles Petersen.

Family members continue to cheer me on in ways both large and small. In the course of writing this book—and for much else besides—I owe most to my wife, Barbara Crouter, my ever sensible and loving companion on life's journey.

CONTENTS

REINHOLD NIEBUHR

I

WHY NIEBUHR IN A NEW ERA?

Many have longed for a new Reinhold Niebuhr to inspire a new generation of religious liberals. I have shared in that longing. But it is doubtful that even Niebuhr could be Niebuhr now. In any event, can you think of a talk show that would book him?

E. J. Dionne, Jr., *Souled Out: Reclaiming Faith and Politics after the Religious Right* (2008)

The war on terror has brought Niebuhr's broader vision into focus: not only the struggle between realism and idealism in our foreign affairs, but the ongoing debate over the place of religion in America's sense of itself. The fresh interest in his work, then, ought to be invigorating—a source of clarity and perspective.

It hasn't been. On the contrary, the Niebuhr revival has been perplexing, even bizarre, as people with profoundly divergent views of the war [in Iraq] have all claimed Niebuhr as their precursor. . . .

Paul Elie, "A Man for All Reasons," *Atlantic* (November 2007)

Liberal and conservative political pundits, journalists, and writers have rediscovered the rich legacy of the premier twentieth-century Protestant theologian and public intellectual Reinhold Niebuhr (1892–1971). A life-long critic of American hubris and overreaching arrogance, Niebuhr was radically dedicated to social justice and the processes of democracy, while resolutely critical of authoritarianism, whether in religion or in politics. Led by the new prominence of Niebuhr's name, diverse Americans are apparently fascinated as well as perplexed by his complex way of plumbing the human condition. His popularity was always greatest among secular opinion-makers, academics, and intellectuals. That situation is echoed today, even if it is less clear to many of these figures how much Niebuhr's central teaching was shaped by the Christian tradition.

The standard labels of "optimist" or "pessimist" are inadequate for Niebuhr, who combines both elements as a self-described "tamed cynic." He is cited by the left as a radical political liberal and by the right as a neoconservative. His reputation as a Christian theologian is both assured and, at the same time, contested. His multiple roles as a teacher of social ethics, preacher, and political activist baffle a public that is eager to know more about his ideas. The prophets of ancient Israel, Jesus of Nazareth, St. Paul, and Augustine inform his Christian vision. He is championed as a one-time socialist, a man of the democratic left, and a relentless advocate of a more just society. But he's also a determined critic of utopian thinking. His political vision is influenced by the study of political philosophy, ranging from the Greeks to seventeenth- and eighteenth-century political theory. Given Niebuhr's tilt toward pessimism, we might think that Machiavelli and Hobbes loom larger in his thought than John Locke's classical liberal politics. In fact, however, he does not endorse the cynicism of *The Prince* (1532) or the authoritarianism of *The Leviathan* (1651). Finally, Niebuhr is a modern, though not uncritical, heir of the sixteenth-century Reformation theologies of Martin Luther and John Calvin, who taught generations of their followers to live by grace alone. Just how his politics and Christian faith relate to one another is a bit of a conundrum for believers and secularists alike.

Early on Niebuhr was aware that his stance does not fit easily into the standard political and religious expectations of modern bourgeois, capitalist America. In the preface to *Reflections on the End of an Era* (1932), written against the backdrop of the First World War and the Depression, he stated: "The effort to combine political radicalism with a more classical and historical interpretation of religion will strike the modern mind as bizarre and capricious."[1] Niebuhr rejected the Manichean habit of thinking there's a sharp, easily distinguishable divide between good and evil. For him, to think that people are purely good or wholly corrupt is not truthful to the human condition. Given the complexity of this stance it's hard to get a handle on him, difficult to gaze steadily into the heart of his thought. Like other strong-minded thinkers, he was surrounded by controversy, misunderstanding, and rival interpretations. Yet Niebuhr's complex insight, conveyed with wit and wisdom, speaks to our inner conflicts as individuals and members of society in the twenty-first century. A primer on the current "Niebuhr revival" on the political left and right, this book traces the ongoing relevance of his ideas for secular as well as for deeply religious minds.

Preacher, Thinker, and Writer

Reinhold Niebuhr's impressive body of editorials, letters, magazine articles, sermons, and books illumine the interplay between religion and political life, between the life of churches and the larger political community. The Manuscript Division of the Library of Congress has some sixty-seven file boxes of Niebuhr papers, correspondence, and memorabilia. Niebuhr worked as a Protestant minister in Henry Ford's Detroit in the 1920s; the thirteen-year apprenticeship in the vagaries of industrial capitalism shaped his reflections on the role of church and on political power in human affairs. He taught Christian social ethics at Union Theological Seminary in New York City from 1928 until his official retirement in 1960. President Henry Sloane Coffin hired the young pastor from the Midwest without a PhD. At the time, Coffin was developing an illustrious faculty with a formidable impact on the education of Protestant clergy. Among Niebuhr's contemporaries on the faculty were the theologian, world churchman, and Coffin's successor as seminary president, Henry Pitney Van Dusen; philosopher-theologian Paul Tillich (1886–1965), whom Niebuhr helped bring to the seminary in 1934 as a refugee from Nazism; and Niebuhr's close collaborator and fellow social ethicist, John C. Bennett, later joined in this field of study by Roger L. Shinn. In 1954 Niebuhr's longtime friend and associate, German-American Reformation historian, Wilhelm Pauck, joined the UTS faculty from the University of Chicago, where he had taught since 1926. Although Niebuhr traveled widely to preach in university chapels, attend ecumenical gatherings of the world church, and form social and political alliances, he dutifully pursued administrative tasks alongside teaching and led in shaping the life of the seminary community.

Along with his brother, H. Richard Niebuhr (1894–1962) at Yale University Divinity School, and his colleague at Union, Paul Tillich, Reinhold Niebuhr dominated academic Protestant theology in the United States in the twentieth century. Influenced by the thought of Ernst Troeltsch (1865–1923), these theologians pursued their own distinctive paths as contemporaries of Karl Barth in Switzerland and Rudolf Bultmann in Germany. Most departments of religion in the colleges and universities in mid- and late-twentieth-century America had at least one faculty member who was influenced by the Niebuhrs and Tillich. Reinhold Niebuhr's books, articles, and sermons were especially influential among Protestant elites and opinion-makers. The more activist of the Niebuhr brothers, his penchant for awakening the churches to the struggle for justice led him to found *Christianity and Crisis* in 1941.[2] The subscriber list of the biweekly "journal of Christian opinion," reached into the highest echelons of government, departments of the universities, and individual homes, as it brought the distinctive form of Niebuhr's "Christian realism" to bear on issues of the day.

Niebuhr's insight into the ambiguity of our human condition—our sense of being surrounded by transcendent mystery, while good and evil impulses struggle within us—informs his books and his many shorter publications. It was his habit to write against the Zeitgeist. When the dark clouds of fascism and Hitler's Germany swept over Europe, he published sermons under the title *Beyond Tragedy,* which suggest that the darkness is real, even as hope reaches beyond despair. When America tilted toward isolationism in 1940–1941, he called for engagement with Britain against the Nazi oppressors, thus departing from his early Christian pacifism and breaking with the liberal Protestant magazine, the *Christian Century,* over this issue. When the United States was victorious in World War II, he published a collection of sermons under the title *Discerning the Signs of the Times,* warning fellow citizens against postwar complacency and a self-congratulatory sense of virtuous accomplishment. Throughout the years he stood steadfastly against cultural panaceas, fashionable trends, and the wishful thinking that reigns in the American marketplace of ideas.

Niebuhr applied his idea of human fallibility to the details of our lives and the unfolding drama of history in endless permutations. In this capacity to range broadly and yet focus sharply, he resembles the description of Leo Tolstoy that the British social philosopher Isaiah Berlin gives in his 1953 book *The Hedgehog and the Fox: An Essay on Tolstoy's View of History.* Berlin took his title from a saying of the ancient Greek poet Archilochus: "The fox knows many things, but the hedgehog knows one big thing." The hedgehog burrows in and sees the world through the lens of a single defining idea, while the fox is constantly on the move, drawing from new experiences. Berlin's depiction of Tolstoy provides apt metaphors for Niebuhr as writer and provocateur. Like the Russian writer, Niebuhr desired "to go to the root of every matter" while holding "an instinctive distrust of the abstract."[3] If Niebuhr's analysis of human fallibility is the work of a hedgehog, his appeal to the facts of experience set forth through the vicissitudes of history attests to the habits of a fox.

Yet for all of Niebuhr's acclaim the fate of his legacy seems to hang in the balance. At the time of his 1992 centenary, observers of American opinion had come to believe that Niebuhr was passé. That belief was bemoaned by admirers and trumpeted by detractors. His demise was further signaled when the journal he founded, *Christianity and Crisis,* ceased publication in 1993. Its pages had significantly departed from the somber agenda fostered by Niebuhrian realism. For critics within the New Left, Niebuhr seemed too tied to cold war thinking in politics, as if he'd mainly been an ideology-driven Cold War hawk. Liberation theologies had in the meantime heralded a new grassroots approach to justice. To a more pluralist America his theological views had not kept up with the waves of feminism, evangelicalism, and shifts of thought within post–Vatican II Roman Catholicism, not to mention the influx of religious diversity and new age faiths. A practicing Christian, lifelong preacher, and churchman, Niebuhr spoke in the cadences of biblical faith and the time-honored vocabulary of liturgical tradition. He did not speak about spirituality or being on a spiritual journey. He knew that Protestant Christian churches were often moribund, dispensed trivialities to their congregants, and were frequently out of touch with social reality. His criticism called for serious political engagement on the part of mainstream Protestantism. He had no experience of today's popular megachurches, emerging churches, or their nondenominational, entertainment-style alternatives. His intellectual sparring partners were Sidney Hook, Paul Tillich, Bertrand Russell, Sigmund Freud, John Dewey, and Billy Graham, not Daniel C. Dennett, Richard Dawkins, Christopher Hitchens, and Rick Warren. As a writer who drew incessantly from time and place, Niebuhr seemed dated and, in some quarters, on the verge of being forgotten.

In the decades following his death in 1971, recurrent laments for Niebuhr and his unique perspective witnessed to his lurking presence in American culture.[4] His advocates regularly called for a return to his teachings. Writing in the *St. Louis Post Dispatch,* June 19, 1992, clergyman Robert Tabscott expressed what others suspected when he observed that Niebuhr's thought "is scarcely discernible in most seminaries and pulpits across the country." That same year Niebuhr's friend, the late historian Arthur Schlesinger, Jr., reminded *New York Times* readers of "Reinhold Niebuhr's Long Shadow," laconically noting that "Niebuhr is currently a subject of acrid dispute between liberals and conservatives, each claiming him."[5] When historian Richard Wightman Fox published a controversial Niebuhr biography in 1985,[6] the event was marked by an exchange between two of Fox's Stanford University teachers. In publishing a face-off between Robert McAfee Brown and Michael Novak in 1986, the *Christian Century* gave voice to rival Niebuhr claimants on the political left and the right.[7] Brown wished to seize Niebuhr for theological liberalism, while Novak had come to see Niebuhr as a father of neoconservatism.

Even then, however, Niebuhr was more than a lurking presence, especially in the academic world. Publication of two more Niebuhr biographies in 1992 by Ronald H. Stone and Charles C. Brown rounded out the legacy and invited fresh interest.[8] His impact was kept alive through the scores of pastors and professors who heard Niebuhr at Union Theological Seminary (1928–1960) or studied elsewhere with those who had done so. A rich body of Niebuhr interpretation continued to unfold. In a cover story in the *Christian Century* (June 7–14, 1995) "Rethinking Reinhold Niebuhr: The Case for Christian Realism," Dennis P. McCann reviewed work by Charles C. Brown, Henry B. Clark, Gabriel Fackre, and Robin W. Lovin.[9]

A further sampling of significant scholarship on Niebuhr would include work by Larry Rasmussen, Edmund N. Santurri, Langdon Gilkey, and further studies by Lovin. Rasmussen's *Reinhold Niebuhr: Theologian of Public Life* (1991) provides a judiciously edited collection of Niebuhr texts; Santurri's work ranges from giving a critical account of Niebuhr on human ambiguity, coercion, and conscience to bringing a Niebuhrian criticism to bear on the political liberalism of John Rawls. Gilkey's *On Niebuhr: A Theological Study* (2001) draws from a lifetime of reflection on Niebuhr, and Lovin's *Christian Realism and the New Realities* (2008) treats the theologian's prospects for a new global order in the twenty-first century.[10]

Nor had Niebuhr been forgotten among political realists who were seeking to shape U.S. strategic thinking. Writing at the end of the Clinton administration, senior *Atlantic* editor Robert D. Kaplan noted that "those who think that America can establish democracy the world over should heed the words of the late American theologian and political philosopher Reinhold Niebuhr."[11] Deeply controversial, sometimes vilified on the question of Islam and the West, the late Samuel P. Huntington, author of *The Clash of Civilizations and the Remaking of World Order* (1996), had, apparently without fanfare, found his own way of appropriating Niebuhr.[12] Finally there is the case of ex-President Jimmy Carter, for whom Niebuhr has been a lifelong influence.[13] If Huntington is driven by the epitome of *Realpolitik,* Carter is the arch-champion of hope beyond the tragedy that seems to rule the world. The ground for rethinking Niebuhr's legacy in the twenty-first century had been quietly prepared, even if frequently off center stage.

Mapping the Niebuhr Revival

In 1986 Harvard University sought a keynote speaker well-suited for its 350th anniversary celebration. American literature professor Alan Heimert, aware of the need for "a public intellectual with a commanding presence who could speak across the disciplines," told President Derek Bok that "only two people in the last twenty years could make that speech—Walter Lippmann and Reinhold Niebuhr—and they both were gone."[14] The present book can be seen as an inquiry into a similar outburst of "Niebuhr nostalgia."

It's not surprising that renewed interest in Niebuhr on politics should have come about during the presidency of George W. Bush. Citations of Niebuhr became especially evident during the problematic Bush presidency, amid the abuse of U.S. power at home and preemptive, imperial adventurism abroad. Diplomatic and military historians and writers on America as a global power are, in varying degree, turning to Niebuhr's criticism of American imperialism. A partial list of such writers includes Gary Dorrien, Niall Ferguson, Michael Ignatieff, Chalmers Johnson, Clyde V. Prestowitz, and Cornel West.[15] Especially prominent in this regard is the work of diplomatic historian Andrew J. Bacevich. Reintroducing Niebuhr's *The Irony of American History* (1952) in a new 2008 paperback edition, Bacevich states that it "is the most important book ever written on U.S. foreign policy."[16] That this is said about the work of a theologian is more than eye-catching. Today it is de rigueur to invoke Niebuhr on the problem of America's overreaching world posture. In general, that is all to the good, even if this response dodges the questions of whether Niebuhr's social and political views are adequately represented and how his robust views of human nature relate to the age-old bedrock of the Christian tradition.

It's no great trick to grasp why Niebuhr has again come to the fore in contemporary America. Based on sales and interest, the book of the moment is *The Irony of American History* (1952).[17] Without mention of Iraq or the Middle East the book gives a penetrating account of America's unwitting, thus ironic, drive toward imperialism. In Niebuhr's hands the analysis of original sin, the tendency toward pretension and moral blindness, illumines the behavior of the nation, not just of individuals. Published at the height of the cold war, the work analyzes how "virtue becomes vice through some hidden defect in the virtue." Irony results when what seems fortuitous is seen, upon reflection, to be not merely fortuitous, but driven by pride and self-interest. Since the 1950s, theologians, historians, and

Americanists have variously assessed the book. Originally panned by some historians as a "neo-Calvinist" attack on liberalism written through a Marxist-Leninist lens, *The Irony of American History* is now read as a critique of U.S. arrogance of power. Its cautionary word applies to all forms of American exceptionalism, including the messianism of John Winthrop's "city set on a hill" speech, which pictures America's path in the world as a steady beacon of light.

Moreover, references to Niebuhr in books, articles, editorials, and internet chatter—often authentic, sometimes serving a writer's extraneous agenda—pop up everywhere today. Writing in the *Atlantic* about lying, journalist Carl Cannon accords Niebuhr a striking place of honor in the phrase "philosophers from Aristotle to Niebuhr have made moral distinctions. . . ."[18] The mere mention of Niebuhr's name adds a touch of gravitas to contemporary opinion. A list of writers on the political left and right who now cite him with approval includes James Fallows, E. J. Dionne, Jr., Peter Beinart, Kevin Mattson, David Brooks, Robert D. Kaplan, and Joseph Loconte.[19] The tug-of-war over Niebuhr, identified by Arthur Schlesinger, Jr., as an acrid debate between left and right, continues in full swing. In contrast to such debates, Anatol Lieven and John Hulsman signal a new stage of Niebuhr reception in their book, *Ethical Realism: A Vision for America's Role in the World* (2006). With a background in think tanks on the left and the right, Lieven and Hulsman join forces in their book to argue for a return to Niebuhr's realism, which, alongside that of Hans J. Morgenthau and George F. Kennan, shaped the policy of containment of the USSR.[20]

Other figures concerned with America's public life and religious vitality are returning to Niebuhr. Since 2005 Krista Tippett's NPR show *Speaking of Faith* has repeatedly highlighted Niebuhr's significance.[21] Former senator from Missouri and U.S. ambassador to the UN John Danforth wrote a senior thesis on Niebuhr as a Princeton undergraduate. He reports that the theologian's impact "had an enormous effect on me, and on how I think about the relationship of Christianity to politics, even though my political views turned out to be significantly more conservative than Niebuhr's."[22]

Veteran PBS television commentator Bill Moyers has a keen sense of the significance of Niebuhr. His show, *Bill Moyer's Journal,* has interviewed persons deeply touched by the thought of Reinhold Niebuhr, including Union Theological Seminary's James Cone, our leading interpreter of black theology, and diplomatic historian Andrew J. Bacevich, both of whom resoundingly endorse the teaching of *The Irony of American History.*[23]

Not surprisingly, Niebuhr's name surfaced in the 2008 U.S. presidential contest. John McCain's campaign biography (with Mark Salter), *Hard Call: The Art of Great Decisions* (2007), devotes an entire chapter to Niebuhr called "the Paradox of War," in a section of the book called, "Humility." The chapter argues that war is awful, though sometimes necessary, while it hints that Niebuhr would have supported the Bush-Cheney war in Iraq. The story of Barack Obama and Niebuhr, a topic of potentially greater yield, remains unfinished. In April 2007, during a dreary moment on the campaign trail, *New York Times* columnist David Brooks "outed" the future president as a Niebuhrian in "Obama, Gospel and Verse."[24] Responding to Brooks's random query about Niebuhr, Obama says, "I love him. He's one of my favorite philosophers," and then summarizes what Niebuhr means to him:

> "I take away," Obama answered in a rush of words, "the compelling idea that there's serious evil in the world, and hardship and pain. And we should be humble and modest in our belief we can eliminate those things. But we shouldn't use that as an excuse for cynicism and inaction. I take away . . . the sense we have to make these efforts knowing they are hard, and not swinging from naïve idealism to bitter realism." [25]

Hunches on how to read Obama as a self-confessed Niebuhrian continue apace. Former George W. Bush speechwriter Michael Gerson weighed in on the topic just before the November 2008 election;[26] it was made legitimate in a *New York Times* article on Obama's reading habits;[27] and it became central to an exchange of views between David Brooks and E. J. Dionne, Jr., at an NPR-sponsored *Speaking of Faith* forum at Georgetown University in January 2009. Much in Obama's hopeful realism echoes Niebuhr's blend of high principles and purposeful pragmatism.

Neither Obama nor Niebuhr lines up easily alongside the standard labels of left or right in politics or in religion. Yet it might be questioned whether the fate of Niebuhr's legacy ought properly to rest with presidential reading habits. A circumspect mind would at least want to weigh the relative import of other writers on the Obama reading list.[28]

Design of the Book

By their own admission Niebuhr's longtime admirers suffer from a degree of nostalgia. Yet asking the wistful question, "What would Reinie do?" has only marginal utility. None of us know for sure what Niebuhr would do or say. We do, however, know a great deal about his stance as a Christian thinker, how he viewed our ambiguous human nature as it relates to crucial questions of political, economic, and religious life. A chance to revisit those ideas is worth more than vague longing for Niebuhr in the flesh. We don't need more factual knowledge about the man. We need a direct encounter with his ideas—the mind of Niebuhr that stands behind the wave of current interest.

Although this inquiry is not biographical, Niebuhr's active life necessarily stands as its backdrop. His biography is among the most significant of his era. When his friend, the Jewish theologian Abraham Heschel, spoke at Niebuhr's June 1971 memorial service he stated, simply and truthfully: "He appeared among us as a figure out of the Hebrew Bible. . . . Niebuhr's life was a song in the form of deeds."[29] It was the highest praise that Heschel, representing a tradition that measures righteousness by its fruits, could give to his Christian friend and colleague. Niebuhr's activism and life of deeds are exemplary and they are intimately connected with his thought.

For present purposes, however, Niebuhr's biography forms the stage upon which his theological and ethical ideas were enacted. This book urges us to ponder the intellectual choices he made amid the twentieth century's storms of life. The popular revival of interest, urged on by needs of the moment, does little to identify Niebuhr's kindred spirits in the history of theology or in the wider world of human letters. The choices he made as thinker and writer reveal his cast of mind above and beyond the details (including the rightness or wrongness) of positions he took over a long career. The times through which he lived do not sufficiently explain the uniqueness of his thought, or its robustness within the trajectory that marks his career. The mind of our greatest theological student of politics and history exceeds the bounds of the crises he analyzed.

In the pages that follow I attempt to explain Niebuhr's thought to nonspecialists without sacrificing intellectual complexity. That's obviously a tall order. Lay and specialist readers will determine the degree to which I have succeeded. It takes nothing away from Niebuhr's originality or achievement if, at the same time, I maintain that the heart of his perspective on human nature (individually and collectively) did not arise completely de novo. His unique way of viewing Christian faith and the political world draws from biblical and theological traditions, as well as from literary, political, and philosophical teachings. Among its other aims this book seeks to place Niebuhr's ideas in the broader stream of cultural and religious history.

Niebuhr's literary output adumbrates a set of tough proposals regarding what Isaiah Berlin, following Kant, calls "the crooked timber of humanity."[30] His quizzical perspective has implications for how we understand ourselves and our fellow humans, and how human life on earth relates to our search for meaning amid moral perplexity. At stake are the issues of where humans stand in a world dominated by science, technology, and rational thought, whether religious values and commitments can and should inform public life, and how our hopes and anxieties as Americans relate to events unfolding in the twenty-first century.

This book treats central tenets of Niebuhr's key texts, including his magnum opus *The Nature and Destiny of Man* (1941, 1943), *Moral Man and Immoral Society* (1932), *The Children of Light and the Children of Darkness* (1944), and *The Irony of American History* (1952). The two-volume Gifford Lectures, *Nature and Destiny,* which followed *Moral Man and Immoral Society,* brought him the national attention that led to his being on the cover of *Time* magazine in March 1948.[31] That a mass news magazine would run seven pages on Niebuhr, while offering background on Dostoevsky, Kierkegaard, and Karl Barth as influences, says much about the reading habits of Americans in the 1940s. The word at the time was that Niebuhr never stopped writing and giving talks. Continuing into the 1960s he regularly contributed articles and commentary to the *Christian Century, Christianity and Crisis,* the *New Leader,* the *New Republic,* the *Reporter,* and the *Atlantic.*

Given the weight and repute of Niebuhr, a revival of interest in his thought is not surprising, even if the shape and extent of that interest could not have been anticipated. In what follows I am more interested in asking *why* all this is happening and *exploring its significance* than in chronicling the fact that it is taking place. A citation index or encyclopedic account of Niebuhr's influence makes dull reading. Instead, I hope to provide an account of his basic ideas that will enable readers to distinguish between what is mistaken among current uses of his name and what is permanent in his wisdom. In the end, this book argues that Niebuhr's fundamental orientation as Protestant Christian theologian and political thinker speaks to issues in today's world, just as it did in his lifetime.

Readers will note that I frequently state questions and put forth concerns in secular as well as in religious language. There are reasons why it is important to do this while giving an exposition of Niebuhr's teaching. Like his early nineteenth-century German predecessor, the liberal Protestant theologian Friedrich Schleiermacher (1768–1834), Niebuhr was constantly engaging and challenging assumptions within the larger culture. In broad terms today's situation has not changed. Whether and how theology speaks to modernity remains a large issue. The global financial collapse that came to a head in 2008–2009 has radically called into question received economic views and causes us to wonder whether a theologian may have a word to say to a world in crisis. Although certain of Niebuhr's critics insist on the incompatibility of Christian belief with secular modes of inquiry, his authority lies in his ability to address issues of concern to believers and skeptics alike. Whether this habit of mind is a fault or a virtue will be argued more thoroughly once we have had a chance to digest more of Niebuhr's ideas.

Admittedly, Niebuhr is an odd figure as an American theologian. Though anchored in an experiential faith, his thought lacks the appeal to emotion we associate with evangelical Protestant preaching. He once stated that the German Evangelical and Reformed Church of his family origins "might best be defined as liberal evangelicalism."[32] Though rooted in a paradigm of human subjectivity, a standard of objective debate about worldly matters is upheld in his work. Though he honors a perspective that arises from the Bible (the Old Testament prophets, the New Testament gospels, and the letters of Paul), he harshly criticizes literalist and fundamentalist religion as obscurantist. Niebuhr's Christianity is more personal and intellectual-polemical than bookish or doctrinal. Yet his views arouse passion and emotion. His thought is more shaped by the temper of Edmund Burke's political philosophy and the spirit of German historical-critical theology than by popular American spirituality.

If Niebuhr were depicting human foibles as a painter, history would be his canvas. An ever-present sense of the past as it impinges upon the present (chapter 2) marks him as almost more European than American. Distant historical figures and movements come alive in his preaching and writing. He teaches us how to learn from the past, while distrusting overly facile historical analogies. His orientation challenges an America that is often indifferent toward the past and congenitally optimistic about the future. By invariably taking the long view Niebuhr sheds light on human possibilities as well as on the immediate challenges we face as a nation.

Niebuhr brings this historical perspective to religion as well as to politics. He is firmly anchored in the classical Christian teaching on human sinfulness (chapter 3). The Christian reading of human nature as sinful has analogies with Greek tragedy, literary classics, and some social-political philosophies. He explores those resemblances, while suspicious of analogy. Most Americans (even many Christians) view sin as antiquated, defeatist, and psychologically unhealthy. Yet an unfazed Niebuhr insists on human nature as sinful. For him human pride—excessive self-preoccupation resulting in moral blindness—is empirical, rooted in the facts of experience. His signature insight holds that the morality of groups (especially of nations) is even less virtuous than that of individuals. His reasoning about this is straightforward: Conscience works less well collectively. Compared to individuals, a group is less free to self-correct its morality. It follows from this idea that the self-interested righteousness and imperialism of a nation, driven by cabals of power, are even more pronounced than the same tendencies in individuals.

It's obvious today that elements of Niebuhr speak directly to America in a time of troubles. But there is an additional reason why he connects with a new audience in the era signified by the election of Barack Obama. By addressing the contradictions in our lives (chapter 4), he makes us aware of illusions. As a writer, Niebuhr is no slouch. He writes demanding prose, yet has the gifts of a talented preacher for connecting with an audience. Though exceptions exist (Kierkegaard, C. S. Lewis, Dorothy Sayers, P. D. James, Marilynne Robinson), we do not generally attribute literary sensitivity to writers of theology.[33] Niebuhr was no poet. But he had an intuitive grasp of powerful language. His frequent aphorisms and arresting phrases make him eminently quotable. His irony and wry humor speak to the self-deceptions and moral conflicts of our lives. As a young Detroit pastor he wrote, "Religious humility is a rarer achievement than religious indifference." While musing on our need for democracy during World War II, he penned the words: "Man's capacity for justice makes democracy possible; but man's inclination to injustice makes it necessary." It's easy to underestimate Niebuhr's gift of being able to connect with words.

No one could have predicted that what some readers consider Niebuhr's great cold war book, *The Irony of American History,* would stand at the center of fresh interest in his work. Without speculating on its future impact, one must admit that *Irony* is already a Niebuhr classic. Chapter 5 treats the complex themes taken up in the reissued book as a case study in his thinking. The points he addresses, and their remedies, apply not just to America. The United States has no monopoly over conflicting political expectations and anguished hopes amid national aspirations. His orientation reflects strong ties to Britain as well as to Germany. Not only was his wife, Ursula Niebuhr, English; but he is also well remembered in the UK for his part in urging the United States to engage with Britain against Hitler. It's worth noting that, despite his considerable ties to his ancestral land's formidable theological tradition, only a handful of his works have been translated into German.[34]

In the end, we need to ask how his Protestant Christian critics and detractors view Niebuhr's understanding of the Christian faith (chapter 6). In a nutshell, we see that his reception today remains ambiguous and his thought contested, just as had occurred in his lifetime. In a larger perspective we see that the history of the Christian tradition is replete with tensions among the patterns that express, interpret, and affirm the faith. His brother, H. Richard Niebuhr, explored these very tensions in his 1951 title, *Christ and Culture.*

Looking at American Protestantism today we see that the progressive evangelical Sojourners movement and publications of its founder, Jim Wallis, illustrate a special case of ambiguity toward Niebuhr. Sojourners Christians share Niebuhr's passion for social justice, even as they seem ambivalent toward Niebuhr's legacy. Without being pacifists on principle, they stand squarely against the tragic conditions that produce and sustain wars. More vociferous is the Niebuhr criticism of Duke Divinity School's theological ethicist Stanley Hauerwas. It is tempting to skip over him as a mere intellectual nuisance to Niebuhrians. But that approach doesn't work for a book that wishes to wrestle with the reception of Niebuhr and prospects for his thought in our day. Named "theologian of the year" by *Time* magazine in 2001, Hauerwas has attained considerable standing in the field of Christian ethics as the self-appointed nemesis of Niebuhr.

Taking a look at Hauerwas enables me to highlight the ways Niebuhr's distinctive voice is rooted in Christian faith and its traditions. In Hauerwas's view Niebuhr was worldly and pragmatic, lacked a church-based theology, and sold out the core of the faith to culture. Ironically, Hauerwas seeks to assume the stance of a critic of comfortable bourgeois religion that earlier motivated Niebuhr. Neither figure is a systematic theologian who treats the full round of Christian teaching. Each of them grasps something authentic within the tradition; their differences, which arise from sets of complex judgments and commitments, are not easily bridged. For his part, Niebuhr deliberately chose to concentrate on Christian anthropology, how the tradition regards human nature. His legacy helps us wrestle not just with politics but also with the teachings of the church and of religious institutions that reach deeply into as well as beyond politics.[35]

Such critics overlook the fact that Niebuhr's sense of radical divine transcendence draws from Judaism and Christianity but has implications for other religions as well. He gives us criteria for reflecting on elements of hope as well as danger within religious traditions, whether Jewish, Christian, Islamic, Hindu, or Buddhist. Religion, he thinks, by its very nature, traffics in absolute claims. It is these that instill faith, hope, and courage in believers. Yet the tendency of religions to foster "true belief" and fanaticism must be challenged. Like the prophets of Israel and the sixteenth-century Protestant reformers Luther and Calvin, Niebuhr maintains that a real deity must be beyond human manipulation. Developing a self-critical, reflective faith is the best antidote for zealotry and idolatrous views of self, society, or the state. Toward that end, he holds that Christian belief is sustained by symbolic (nonliteral) speech and history-evoking rituals. The moral imperative of the law of love requires Christians to engage the world in the struggle for social justice, while continually being reminded by the teaching of Jesus that the way forward involves self-knowledge and risks being morally hazardous.

As in all inquiries, we need to ask what all this amounts to for ourselves as readers. It's one thing to admire Niebuhr's words and ideas but quite another to imagine oneself living with his sober insight in the world he depicts. Chapter 7 takes up the question of what it is like to live with Niebuhr's legacy. What is the relevance of his teaching for our lives today? Does his legacy speak not just politically, but Christianly, in today's world? His ideas acknowledge the tragic dimension of our existence, tempered by religious faith and an ironic sense of our place in the cosmos. Religions speak to their practitioners at more than a single level, and they do so deliberately. Like other faiths, Christianity recognizes suffering and imperfection as the hallmarks of our existence; Christianity is not a cult of happiness and unadulterated joy. At the same time Niebuhr's realism recognizes the goodness ("common grace") of the created order, a sense of life's possibilities that undergird every moment. That is the warrant for our having a sense of hope. Niebuhr's insistence that we live with a new sense of limits accords with themes and goals of contemporary ecology. To engage with his persistent voice is to be challenged by a new critical self-awareness. That process may also cause us to revise how we think about religion, about our nation, and about world affairs. If we adopt Niebuhr's way of thinking, we will attend to the demands of morality, while aware of our limited place in the larger scheme of things.

Niebuhr's stance is morally engaged, biblically informed, and ecumenically Christian, and it stands close to the prophets of ancient Israel. Like his critics, he can be polemical and occasionally caustic. Niebuhr holds that Christians do not have a monopoly on worldly wisdom. But neither do the most outspoken champions of atheism. Whether acknowledging or denying God, believers, seekers, atheists, and agnostics all appeal to a shared sense of morality. Our moral beliefs stand beneath a higher order; philosophers and theologians call it a "transcendental" order of good. Whether acknowledged as "a foundational given" or as the "God-given mystery of the universe," the morality to which we appeal has been discovered, more than invented, by humans. Without this radically transcendent (nonempirical) sense of good, viewed through secular eyes or through a deep faith, politics remains a messy form of tribal or national religion.

In wrestling with moral questions Niebuhr's way of arguing is more contextual and rhetorical than systematic and philosophical. He was not a metaphysician. Like most of us, Niebuhr knew in his heart that we must affirm and appeal to a higher moral order amid the daily challenges of our individual and collective lives. What gives depth to his teaching is the constant appeal to history and the facts of our experience as limited humans who are surrounded by the crises of a troubled and perplexing world.

2

TAKING THE LONG VIEW OF HISTORY

The lectures were eventually collected in two volumes titled The Nature and Destiny of Man (1941, 1943). After you've finished a book with a title like that, what's left to read?

David Brooks, "A Man on a Gray Horse," *Atlantic,* September 2002

Krista Tippett: "I guess I have to wonder whether Niebuhr is simply too complex a thinker for our time, whether this kind of nuance and this sense of irony, paradox and attention that you don't try to resolve, but decide to live with and live into. Is there a place for that in American life, in the 21st century?"

Jean Bethke Elshtain: "We're in very big trouble if there isn't."

From the NPR show *Speaking of Faith,* "Moral Man and Immoral Society: The Public Theology of Reinhold Niebuhr," February 10–15, 2005

Times of crisis often provoke sweeping insight. They provoke us to think big ideas that go beyond the daily headlines. St. Augustine's *City of God* arose in an effort to defend Christians against charges of being responsible for the decline of Rome after the fifth-century Germanic invasions. Arnold Toynbee's multivolume *A Study of History* monumentally tries to grasp the rise and fall of civilizations at a time when Britain was patently losing its empire.[1] Such works arise in history as a mind struggles to make sense of the contours of the world—points when civilization as we know it stands on the brink of disaster. The crises of the twentieth century—economic collapse, depression, world wars, recovery, and the cold war between rival ideologies—provoked large thoughts in the mind of Niebuhr. Similarly, the domestic and international crises of our own moment in history attune our minds to ask what we might again learn from Niebuhr.

Reflection on human nature and history in a time of extreme crisis constitutes the subject of Niebuhr's magnum opus, *The Nature and Destiny of Man,* delivered in Edinburgh during the spring and fall of 1939. As he spoke in Scotland, a foreboding sense of war was in the air. By hindsight we see that Niebuhr's two sets of lectures on human nature and the meaning of history framed the Nazi invasion of Poland that launched the Second World War in September. When published after an interval of several years, the work fell upon American Protestants like a theological manifesto. Its lofty themes call for a return to the teachings of St. Paul, Augustine, and Kierkegaard as a counterweight to modern optimism. The Christian view of man, Niebuhr argues, challenges the assumptions about the human condition of both classical Greek and modern European forms of idealism and rationalism.

Niebuhr's two-volume book argues that sinful humanity lives simultaneously in history and nature, thus combining a sense of freedom and biological givenness in an unstable combination of self-awareness and natural existence. Not recognizing the precariousness of human existence, well-understood in biblical and theological traditions, modern civilization lives and shapes its politics based on illusions about individual and collective forms of human selfhood. Volume one of *Nature and Destiny* presents Niebuhr's Christian anthropology, while volume two treats human destiny, millenial expectations, the Kingdom of God, and the end of history in theological perspective. His ideas about human nature also involve how we relate to time: our sense of past, present, and future. For him, history is the stage upon which the drama of our human nature plays out. Niebuhr's sense of history is the broadest, most pervasive aspect of his thought. His central thematic elements, the human self and the drama of history, are thoroughly interwoven.

It's obvious that Niebuhr's lifework reflects this preoccupation with history. His activism as a pacifist in the 1920s, a member of the Socialist Party until 1940, a founder of Americans for Democratic Action in 1947, and columnist for the *Nation,* the *Christian Century,* the *New Leader,* and *Christianity and Crisis* attests to his engagement with history. Niebuhr's second book, the diary of a pastor in Detroit, *Leaves from the Notebook of a Tamed Cynic* (1929), pondered the complacencies of acculturated religion as he sought to find a voice amid the social-economic struggles of Henry Ford's Detroit, long before the rise of trade unions, in the days of the unfolding depression. On the national stage, Niebuhr decried the rapacious greed of capitalism in "Awkward Imperialist," published in the *Atlantic* (May 1930). National correspondent James Fallows noted in 2006 that the piece may be "the most eerily timely" of reflections on America published in the *Atlantic* over the previous 150 years.[2] In that article Niebuhr argues that America cloaks its economic power, achieved through German reparations ($1.9 billion) and debt to the U.S. ($1.2 billion), through the pretense of justly punishing a Weimar Germany that was already falling apart. For Niebuhr our imperialism as a nation arises from impulses of national pride and arrogance. Militarily we had not yet come of age. He did not first see America's arrogance in statecraft arising as a result of victory in World War II, let alone coming into being with the buildup to the 2003 Iraq war.

History-laden themes permeate Niebuhr's publications. *Nature and Destiny* was neither its beginning nor its end. Little read today, *Reflections on the End of an Era* (1932) takes stock of America at the dawn of FDR's New Deal. A collection of sermons under the title *Beyond Tragedy: A Christian Interpretation of History* (1937) originated during the depression and the rise of Hitler's Germany. They vividly illustrate the perilous confusion that surrounds a disastrous mixing of religion and politics. A 1937 sermon on "The Ark and the Temple" protests against the Davidic monarchy, while warning against the idolatry that gives divine sanction to acts of war. It was Niebuhr's way of attacking the misuse of God to sanction human violence. A sermon on the biblical "Tower of Babel" (Genesis 11: 1–9) takes the ancient mythical account of the origins of the world's languages as metaphor for human pretension. Our towers, he thinks, become "Towers of Babel" when they "pretend to reach higher than their real height" and "claim a finality which they cannot possess."[3] Such sermons are not just political in the sense of focusing upon foes of America. They aim at the pretension that clings to our actions and self-understanding as a righteous people. The sermonic essays *Discerning the Signs of the Times* (1946) urge America to learn to live "between the times" and to temper its sense of virtue with realism following the defeat of Germany and Japan.

Deepening an awareness of how history shapes our lives was a constant preoccupation for Niebuhr. Specialists in his thought typically see his later works on history, *Faith and History* (1949), *The Self and the Dramas of History* (1955), and *Pious and Secular America* (1958) as repetitive, hence less novel and compelling. But that reaction misses the point. As mid-twentieth-century reprises of Niebuhr on Niebuhr, they embellish and confirm his lifelong effort to understand and interpret the past, further nuanced by unfolding events in his own day. Taken together, these books comprise Niebuhr's post–World War II search for meaning in history; cast Martin Buber's great theme of dialogue (from his book *I and Thou*) into a Niebuhrian mold; and reprint a series of essays that convey Niebuhr's views on how Christians relate to Jews, how America relates to Russia, how we all relate to higher education, and how a sense of mystery relates to the quest for meaning in our lives.

Why History Matters

To ask generally why history matters seems unusual in a book that treats politics, religion, and the Christian faith. That is less the case if we are willing to explore why it mattered so much to Niebuhr. Admittedly, the significance of having a sense of history, of wondering how we fit into the larger human saga, isn't immediately obvious. We're aware that time passes and moves us toward the future. If we think about it, we become aware that time is not experienced uniformly. Typically we remember the highs and lows of our experience: the instances of great joy and sorrow in our individual lives, our families, or the life of our nation. Such points of orientation give us a sense that we belong to a wider human story. Our lives as rational, naturally evolving, human beings play out in an eventful, time-laden scheme of things.

Being willing to think such thoughts nudges us closer to Niebuhr's world. For him, the unfolding of history alongside the evolving natural order is basic to what we are as humans. History constitutes the broad field of our experience as humans. To borrow a phrase used by his brother, H. Richard Niebuhr, "We are in history as fish are in water."[4] All of the obdurate questions and anxieties that we confront in the realms of politics and religion arise in our history. If history is the arena in which we live, a rhetoric laced with irony and wry wit is his vehicle of discernment.

Reinhold Niebuhr's quasi-European sense of history adds depth and perspective to his reflection. He disdains the eighteenth-century Enlightenment's meta-narrative of humanity's inevitable progress. Yet he knows the hold of that narrative over the American character. The First World War and illusions of Wilsonian foreign policy indelibly shaped the young German-American Protestant minister during 1912–1928. He was aware that many Americans, like Britons prior to 1914–1918, thought of the nineteenth century as an era of peace and prosperity. Of course, this sentiment, tied to the alleged permanence and security of the British Empire, flew in the face of the Franco-Prussian war as well as the racial and national crisis of the U.S. Civil War.

Niebuhr's life experience taught him that history was full of conflict and a struggle for survival, whether on battlefields of France or in the early industrial capitalism of Henry Ford's Detroit. Throughout his life he challenged the modern liberal, optimistic worldview with a call for a greater sense of realism regarding the human condition. To his mind, having a historical perspective was the best way to gain and to retain that sense of realism.

If Niebuhr was not alone in taking this position, his was its most persistent voice among contemporary Christian theologians. It was impossible for him to view the social conflicts, upheavals, and injustices of history as supporting optimistic conclusions. Horror-filled atrocities and genocides of his day, which continue in the twenty-first century, also lead to questioning the idea of progress. By taking the long view, Niebuhr sees history as full of contradictions, surprises, self-deceptions, and reversals of expectations. His views offer a special challenge to Americans as a forward-looking people who may be unaware of how much the past, often half-consciously, impinges upon and provides clues to the present.

Untrained as a professional historian, Niebuhr was a self-taught interpreter of the past. Working historians sometimes think he paints with too broad a brush. For him, however, history (like theology) is too important to be relegated to the tidy monographs and footnotes of professionals. He tends to view scholarship as muting the urgency of honest debate. David Bromwich describes Niebuhr as a master at the "condensed paraphrase" of positions he admires as well as those he rejects, thus producing a "capsule narrative of intellectual debates juxtaposed with recent historical events."[5] As a writer Niebuhr preferred deft summary and argumentative dissonance.

If history has significance, thinking about it requires writers with insight and imagination beyond what is needed to write tidy monographs. A tendency to resist generalizations about the past—sometimes about anything at all[6]—has recently been on the increase. Literary critics, social scientists, and philosophers wonder whether we can speak intelligently about a human nature, apart from our biological makeup. In contrast to this caution the habit of taking bold intellectual risks was characteristic of Niebuhr. He debated the issues of the day amid a generation of towering intellects in American letters that included Walter Lippmann, Jacques Barzun, Lionel Trilling, and Lewis Mumford. In the end, Niebuhr's analyses of the twists and turns of history attracted as many historians as they repelled. Foremost among admirers was the late Arthur Schlesinger, Jr., who supplied a page of helpful comments on the typescript of *The Irony of American History,*[7] and subsequently dedicated the first volume of his magisterial *The Age of Roosevelt* to the Protestant theologian.[8] In his final *New York Times* op-ed,

"Folly's Antidote," (January 1, 2007), Schlesinger wrote (without naming Niebuhr): "History is the best antidote to delusions of omnipotence and omniscience. Self-knowledge is the indispensable prelude to self-control, for the nation as well as the individual, and history should forever remind us of the limits of our passing perspectives."[9] The words stand as a virtual précis of the present chapter's argument. Schlesinger's view that self-knowledge can alleviate our folly recurs in subsequent pages of this book.

The Prophetic Perspective

A preacher by trade before he became a public figure, Niebuhr's thought is steeped in the realistic way that biblical narratives, images, metaphors, and perspectives address the human condition. Putting matters this way risks being misunderstood. Many Americans don't think of the Bible as a resource for serious moral reflection. The Ten Commandments and teachings of Jesus ("love your neighbor as yourself") seem admirable. But the moral authority of scripture (both Old and New Testaments) is radically questioned, both because of doubts about the biblical God, and because objectionable moral practices are enjoined (holy war, genocide, condemnations of homosexuality, to name a few). Like other post-Enlightenment theologians, Niebuhr no longer reads scripture as a divine law book. His historical-critical approach wrestles with biblical teaching contextually. In drawing insight from the Bible, Niebuhr is not a literalist. For him, biblical faith is expressed within the human stories and struggles conveyed by the text's writers, through the poetry and narratives of a people who stand in a dynamic relationship with a transcendent deity. The prophets of Israel were real figures; their pronouncements challenged reigning political authorities as well as their own people. Like Niebuhr, the prophets of Israel have an acute sense for detecting moral obtuseness and hypocrisy.

The work done by prophets has more to do with the present than we often acknowledge, even if they aim at promoting righteous goals that lie ahead. In one respect, they do what Frank Rich of the Sunday *New York Times* does, even if Rich might find it ridiculous to be likened to a biblical prophet. Such figures peer more deeply into the behind-the-scenes forces that shape history than do most people, and they do so through a strong moral lens. Yet they are not lawgivers or arbiters. They appeal to a certain standard of morality as a given. In Abraham Heschel's words: "The prophetic utterance, therefore, has no finality. It does not set forth a comprehensive law, but a single perspective. It is expressed *ad hoc,* often *ad hominem,* and must not be generalized."[10] It's not far off the mark to say they are like journalists whose sense of urgency and moral outrage turns them (sometimes reluctantly) into writers of op-ed pieces, timely articles, and books. In fact, that's a fair description of Niebuhr in action.

For biblical religion human struggles unfold in a linear perspective between alpha and omega, between a mythic beginning and an end that has not yet arrived. The Bible's moral experience thus frames itself through time and history. The prophetic view sees the unfolding of history as a mysterious process of reversals and new beginnings. Israel was not a nation of individuals, but a corporate entity. What befalls one person has implications for the people as a whole and for their neighbors, both nearby and far away. The prophets specialize in discerning the underlying meaning of a people's history, on the basis of which a people is held to account. For prophets like Amos, Isaiah, or Jeremiah, good fortune shall never be taken for granted as deserved, while bad fortune may show immediate divine judgment, even as it points the way toward divine mercy. How the prophets stand in the midst of history is never simplistic. The truth that they set forth captures the divine pathos: a higher, moral perspective that illumines present despair as well as future hope. Abraham Heschel makes clear that the prophets of ancient Israel pronounce more about having a right relationship with God than about laws and principles. The prophet's "sense of election and personal endowment is overshadowed by his sense of a history-shaping power."[11]

Let's try to be clear about what all this means. The prophets of Israel typically bring a divinely inspired word of judgment that bears directly on contemporary affairs. "Thus says the Lord. . . . and I spoke. . . ." But they are scarcely puppets in the hands of deity. Their distinctive voices and emotional commitment as individuals are seen in their words. When the prophet Nathan confronts King David as murderer and adulterer, he tells him a parable about a rich man who took a poor man's one little ewe lamb. When David condemns such a fellow, Nathan famously pronounces: "Thou art the man" (2 Samuel, chapter 12). The story arouses us as an exposé of hypocrisy in high places. To understand its meaning requires a sense of right and wrong that the Bible presupposes. The story doesn't appeal to miracles or supernatural events. Niebuhr's views and pronouncements, as a modern preacher and political actor, do not purport to represent "the word of the Lord" literally. Yet the act of preaching mediates God's mercy and judgment to a congregation. It would be a mistake not to recognize that he speaks and writes from a sense of moral and religious pathos that stands in judgment of the false security and sense of self-righteousness that are endemic in human affairs. He shares with the prophets of ancient Israel a sense that historical outcomes are finally beyond human control. As mortals, perfection lies beyond us, even, sometimes especially, when our leaders are among the most talented and virtuous on earth.

In Niebuhr's mind past dilemmas inform issues in the present. The books, sermons, and articles that he wrote from the 1920s through the 1960s touch upon history as it was being played out under his nose. What he says is shaped for specific occasions amid particular contexts. The events in question may be as small as a particular civil rights bill before the U.S. Congress or as large as a threatening ideology, like Nazism or Communism, as troubling as the balance of nuclear terror or as annoying as zealous expressions of personal righteousness. Since he speaks to specific moments, Niebuhr's thought is conditioned by time. But the content of what he says, by appealing to an overriding, nonrelativist moral perspective, transcends the ebb and flow of our existence. It's what Isaiah was talking about when he wrote, "The flower fades, the grass withers . . . but the Word of the Lord endures forever." Nathan used this standard to view and to weigh the drama of human existence with consistent moral discernment.

History as Mirror of the Self

As we reflect more on Niebuhr, we discover even more practical reasons why it's important to have a sense of history. We deepen our experience of history through encounters with ideas and events that reflect our stories, told in other times and places. We do this amid our present surroundings. Coming to grips with history deepens our grasp of present reality, while chastening our specific hopes for the future. The ancient Roman statesman Cicero saw this clearly when he wrote that "not to know any history is to forever remain a child."[12] Of course, one can remain skeptical about the usefulness of the past. Sometimes we want to agree with the nineteenth-century philosopher Hegel that

> what experience and history teach is that peoples and governments have never yet learned from history, let alone acted according to its lessons. . . .

> In the turmoil of world affairs no universal principle, no memory of similar conditions in the past can help us—a vague memory has no power against the vitality and freedom of the present. [13]

Unlike Hegel, Niebuhr viewed the insight of history as yielding neither "universal principles" or resting on "vague memories." To him history wasn't a guidebook to the workings of reason so much as a vast tapestry of lessons regarding human ambition and foibles. Yet even Hegel's skepticism about history was not the last word for the Berlin philosopher. He set forth an entire philosophy of world history that sought to throw light on human development reaching up to his own present moment.

Cicero was right to observe that history functions to extend our conscious awareness. Drawing insight from the past makes us more self-aware. We weigh and learn from beliefs and behaviors that occurred before we were born. This habit of mind can liberate us from being imprisoned by intellectual fashions and current ideologies. By pointing to other possibilities it frees us from the constraints of racial, religious, or even national identities. Getting to know Niebuhr's thought may free us from stereotypes of religion and politics. That's presumably why we enjoy reading authors from other times and places. In the activity of reading, they are no longer dead. For Niebuhr, confronting historical experience yields a sober sense of our plight as well as our prospects.

Niebuhr's *Nature and Destiny* can be seen as an effort to engage the past while extending and refining his account of Christian self-awareness. Its ideas had special urgency for Western civilization that was directly threatened by a militaristic dictatorship. Facing the Third Reich as a German-American, Niebuhr probed the philosophical past, the history of Christian theology, and the insight of the Bible. As he sifted through reflection on human nature of ancient, medieval, and modern periods, Niebuhr arbitrated between debates regarding reason, tradition, and aspirations of Western culture. His views draw on classical teachings of the Christian tradition, especially about human sinfulness and grace, the promise and meaning of Christ's redemption, alongside the false alternatives propounded by the secular culture and by religious dogmatists and obscurantists. At times an arduous read, the themes of *Nature and Destiny* are artfully interwoven to advance the book's overall perspective. The two volumes are not about history in an external way. They challenge us to think about our own history and how the Christian view of the self relates to alternative ways of depicting humanity.

The work's first sentence, "Man has always been his own most vexing problem," makes it clear that the human is indeed a curious sort of animal.[14] What this sentence means is further explored in chapter 3 with the help of St. Paul, Augustine, and Kierkegaard. For now, it will suffice to say that Niebuhr drew analogies from intellectual history in order to argue against forms of rationalism that overemphasize the power of human reason as well as the modern, post-Renaissance view of individual autonomy that leads to inevitable human progress and human perfectibility. Without being dismissive, he questions the adequacy of the philosophical views of Plato, Aristotle, and the Stoics. With its supreme confidence in reason the eighteenth-century Enlightenment attempted to return to the classical view, while the progress of science, in its grasp of the secrets of nature, contributed to this sense of mastery and control over our destiny.

However, if rationalism puts too much confidence in reason, the view of human life as rooted mainly in natural existence falls short in the other direction. Elsewhere in his work Niebuhr associated naturalism with writers as diverse as John Dewey with his pragmatic philosophy and Sigmund Freud in the practice of psychoanalysis. Such thinkers, he believed, sought to account for and correct human behavior on the basis of natural processes that can be analyzed scientifically. But if rationalism overemphasized the triumph of reason, naturalism (today "naturalism" is used mainly for modern neuroscience and biology) saw the human mainly as a product of the evolutionary process that can, in part, be affected by reason. If the classical worldview stressed our supreme reason, the modern view sees us as more irrevocably tied to, and determined by, natural processes.

Using the terms "rationalism" and "naturalism" as catchwords for contemporary stances of intellectual history allowed Niebuhr to pull together his main thesis. That thesis goes something like this: In contrast with the view of rationalism (which emphasizes our ability to reason) and naturalism (which stresses our organic, biological makeup and needs), the Christian view of human nature, which Niebuhr traces back through St. Augustine to St. Paul, rests on a different assessment of the constitutive elements of our nature. The classical Greeks saw clearly that we consist of mind (or soul) and of body. But for Niebuhr, drawing from Christian sources, the human consists fundamentally of mind, body, and will, a dynamic entity that has the potential for good, even as the self is haunted by moral perplexity. Niebuhr is most concerned to move the discussion of human nature away from soul-body or mind-body dualisms. (He rarely uses the term "soul" and prefers to speak of the human as a "self" which consists of the ever-present mingling of mind, will, and body.[15]) It's worth noting that, for him, no activity of mind is devoid of intention or human will; our having intentions seems to be built-in. Hence for Augustine to construe the will as primary seems cogent to him. Niebuhr sees us as fragile, ever-shifting combinations that are determined as well as free, shaped by nature as well as free to rise above that natural condition to pursue our dreams and to try to attain the good life, individually and collectively. Expressed in biblical language, we are both creators and creatures.

Alongside the human will, our minds and bodies remain intact. There is little patience in Niebuhr for the time-honored efforts to reduce the human to mind (as if our bodies don't exist) or to our bodies (as if our minds are not also real). His view that we are a wondrous mix of the mental and the biological continues to resonate within contemporary neural science. Moreover, Niebuhr is as suspicious of extreme flights of mysticism as he is of appeals to a consistent materialism. Mysticism in its various forms (whether secular or within religious traditions) loses the connection between self and world and denies the fundamental biblical view of the goodness of creation, including individuals. If mysticism were a valid alternative, then political options and striving for a more just world would be superfluous. For Niebuhr, mysticism is mainly seen as an escape from our worldly responsibilities. At the same time, to represent the human as nothing more than materiality or biological impulses similarly reduces humanity to a single dimension and denies our complexity.

The Enigma of Consciousness

Niebuhr would lack relevance if his key ideas did not connect with debates in our day. How then, we may ask, does his account of human uniqueness stand up in today's world? We've seen how his long view of history enabled him to compare and contrast rival ways that philosophers and scientists portray the human condition. That process led him to the view of the human animal as unique in the sense of being "a self that is aware of itself."

> The rationalists do not always understand that man's rational capacity involves a further ability to stand outside himself, a capacity for self-transcendence, the ability to make himself his own object, a quality of spirit that is usually not fully comprehended or connoted in . . . any of the concepts which philosophers usually use to describe the uniqueness of man.[16]

We need not be alarmed or embarrassed by the term "self-transcendence," which is still in use by theologians and philosophers. It has nothing to do with ESP or rising above one's humanity into another sphere—claimed areas of experience that awakened Niebuhr's suspicion, if not his ire. What Niebuhr means, and does not mean, by "the uniqueness of man" is more subtle. But first we do well to note that his rejection of purely mentalist or materialist accounts of human nature is defended by contemporary philosophers.

In *The Mystery of Consciousness* (1997), John R. Searle debates philosophers who wish to eliminate consciousness as "ethereal" or "mystical." He notes that

> all these reductionist attempts to eliminate consciousness are as hopeless as the dualism they were designed to supplant. In a way they are worse, because they deny the real existence of the conscious states they were supposed to explain. They end up by denying the obvious fact that we all have inner, qualitative, subjective states such as our pains and joys, memories and perceptions, thoughts and feelings, moods, regrets, and hungers.

Niebuhr would not deny Searle's main claim that "consciousness is a natural, biological phenomenon. It is as much a part of our biological life as digestion, growth, or photosynthesis."[17] But the human animal ("the self") has a curious feature above and beyond the account given by John Searle. What is, for Niebuhr, vexatious about the human condition arises not from specific subjective states of awareness (pains, joys, moods, etc.) but from the fact that we are more generally "conscious of our consciousness." Our uniqueness, for Niebuhr, arises from the fact that our inner musings lead us to wonder why we, or humans generally, are subject to pain, joy, rapidly fluctuating moods, and the like. What is the sense, we may ask, of being so constituted? Being moved in that direction—Niebuhr believes we are all so moved at some points of our lives—often initiates a new quest for meaning, where answers are apt to lie in poetry, music, literature, the arts, or religious faith. Whatever the incredible progress being made in mapping the brain, neural science is far from giving a biological account of the wonderment and self-bewilderment at the heart of such questions. To say that the human is special in this way doesn't mean that the human is special in all respects. Our being a unique part of the earth's ecosystem doesn't give us dominion over all else. Being different humanly consists of being aware of the peculiarity of our selfhood. This "consciousness of self-awareness" exceeds what we mean by reasoning. It includes the ability to make choices freely, which in Niebuhr's biblical language is "the image of God in man" (Genesis 1: 26–27).

This capacity for self-transcendence drew Niebuhr to admire the seventeenth-century philosopher Blaise Pascal, who wrote about the "grandeur and the misery" of man (*Pensées* 418):

> It is dangerous to make man see too clearly his equality with the brutes without showing him his greatness. It is also dangerous to make him see his greatness too clearly, apart from his vileness. It is still more dangerous to leave him in ignorance of both. But it is very advantageous to show him both. Man must not think that he is on a level either with the brutes or with the angels, nor must he be ignorant of both sides of his nature; but he must know both.

The combination of our freedom and our capacity of self-transcendence means that humans can conjure up great schemes of good and evil, projects of sheer altruism and gratuitous cruelty, that are unheard of to the same degree among other animals. We have a capacity to do higher mathematics and theoretical physics as well as to invent and use weaponry and chemicals to destroy innocent life, our own and the rest of the ecosystem. All of this is implied in the opening line of *Nature and Destiny:* "Man has always been his most vexing problem."

The point about self-transcendence was made anecdotally in a 1952 Niebuhr talk called "The Christian Faith and Humanism." There he relates that a biologist in a southern university had written him to say that she finally has proof that there is no difference between humans and the other animals, since she has discovered that she can teach her canaries to sing each other's songs. He reports that he wrote to the biologist to say that he'd be more impressed if she could show him a bird that had written the history of music.[18] Of course, Niebuhr might also have wondered whether a canary could teach things to its biologist owner. An anecdote is not a formal argument. But in the midst of intellectual debates, stories have a place.

Though the language and levels of sophistication have changed, the poles of the debate about human nature remain largely in place. Niebuhr's defense of a middle ground that includes a psycho-physical but willing self comes alive when we ponder the battles in our own time between those who insist that the human has some unique capacities and those who assert that we are nothing but the sum of our brain waves. The problem will very likely persist, even if we believe that Niebuhrian "self-transcendence" is the summation of our very considerable biological makeup. It takes more than having a foundation in biology to turn the troubled human animal into a harmonious entity, totally in sync with itself.

As creatures within the evolutionary cycle, we share in the fate of all plants and animals. Yet we live in a realm of history where we shape human affairs in ways that impinge on the entire planet. The complex interplay of causality and contingency cuts across the realms of nature as well as in history. As humans, the nexus between what we do and are by nature and what we do and become in history occupies the best minds of scientists and poets among us. The rub comes when we realize that we have the capacity to intervene in human affairs and the fate of the earth, while being unsure whether we have the intellectual ability, moral will, and practical wisdom to act wisely and to assume responsibility for the consequences of our actions.

The Experience of Contingency

There's another lesson about history where Niebuhr's ideas speak to today's world. This concerns our experience of the quirky and unpredictable (philosophers call it contingent) nature of historical events. Contingency, which we often perceive as chance, seems to play a much larger role in our lives and that of our nation than we are eager to acknowledge. Forces at work in history are vastly complex and unfold in surprising ways, defying the best experts of the day. It's easy to make the point in connection with the 2008 election of a multiethnic Barack Obama and the collapse of global financial markets. In both cases we were reliably told that such things could not possibly happen in our day, the one because racial prejudice forbids it, and the other because the expertise of government officials and enlightened self-interest of investors no longer allows it.

This discussion of contingency is captured in one of Niebuhr's pithy aphorisms. Coming out of retirement in 1967 to address students in the Social Hall of Union Theological Seminary on the folly of the Vietnam War, Niebuhr, in his slightly gravelly voice, intoned the words: "History always repeats itself, but never in the same way."[19] To tidy minds the saying sounds like a logical conundrum. Either history repeats itself, we think, or it doesn't. Against a seemingly innocent truth Niebuhr goes for complexity. There's enough repetition in the dramas of history for us to grasp similarity, but enough novelty to throw off exact repetition, let alone an ability to predict. This is why historical analogies are so often misused in the service of ideological objectives. It's foolish to equate the Iraq war with Vietnam unless we also analyze the differences. It's also foolish to see the financial meltdown of 2008 as a repeat of 1929 unless we also look at dissimilarities, of which there are plenty. That said, another level of analogy keeps the events together. In both instances these unheralded events shock a troubled nation and throw normal expectations off track.

It was the artistry of Niebuhr's persistent social and political criticism, but also his religious and theological writing, to discern similarity amid difference within the unfolding drama of human history. Ever since Plato's *Phaedrus,* professional philosophers have referred to this art of discerning unity within difference as dialectics.[20] Others are content just to name it as a talent for making lucid comparative judgments, the kind that preserve tensions without falling into exaggeration. Whatever we may wish to call it, talent in this art of moral discernment made Niebuhr among the most probing thinkers of his era.

Even when its continuing themes are obvious, history constantly moves forward, thus betraying its transient nature. If we miss this sense of history as a series of permanent transitions, we shall miss Niebuhr altogether. That view contrasts with a popular impression that the present really exists (that's what we see, feel, and hear), the past is fleeting (we have to work to gather it in), and the future is wholly unknown. For Niebuhr, history's drama unfolds freely as a series of infinitely complex acts. That is true of the present, but also of the past and the future. Because of history's contingent nature, it is indecipherable and unpredictable.

As a critic of George W. Bush's policies, Andrew J. Bacevich reminds us that history is incapable of being stage-managed by humans.[21] On this point Niebuhr is a polemicist; he attacks the pretension of modern ways of knowing that purport to control and manage our destiny. The matter at hand is related to the debate in philosophical textbooks between freedom and determinism. We are incapable of deciding whether history is a causal chain, or whether it is open-ended, full of possibilities. Too often we approach history as if what happened had to happen just as it did. Holding this tacit belief obscures the fact that events might well have turned out differently.

Rational choice theory in social science and modern economics rests on the view that, given our freedom, we will choose what is in our interest. Of course, the idea of rational self-interest breaks down if you hold, as Niebuhr did, that self-interest and pride cloud our vision of what is truly rational. Endorsing St. Augustine's view of the human condition, he wrote: "Man is a curious creature with so strong a sense of obligation to his fellows that he cannot pursue his own interests without pretending to serve his fellowmen."[22] The Augustinian sentiment, far from being cynical, stands as a mantra of realism. It fits the recent champions of trickle-down economics and dot-com bubbles, to say nothing at all about the marketing of Ponzi schemes. For Niebuhr pride and ego fool us into believing our choices are enacted in the interest of others. As Plato taught long ago in the *Cratylus,* self-deception is the worst sort of deception, for "the deceiver is always at home and always with you."[23]

It is perhaps fortuitous that secular writers are now also documenting how our perceptual biases shape behavior. It almost looks as if statisticians and social scientific observers are catching up with what Niebuhr takes to be sinful, self-regarding views of ourselves that are not drawn from "the facts of experience." The work of mathematician and financial trader Nassim Nicholas Taleb, *Fooled by Randomness: The Hidden Role of Chance in Life and in the Markets* (2004), is a case in point.[24] In a *New York Times* column David Brooks cites Taleb on the folly of risk-management models used on Wall Street:

> Taleb is characteristically vituperative about the quantitative risk models, which try to model something that defies modelization. He subscribes to what he calls the tragic vision of humankind, which believes in the existence of inherent limitations and flaws in the way we think and act and requires an acknowledgment of this fact as a basis for any individual and collective action.[25]

Taleb's thought underscores in secular language the ways that our efforts to exert full control over our lives fly in the face of the apparent randomness that is perceived by statisticians.

A related point about our ability to control and the illusions it creates is found in Malcolm Gladwell's *Outliers: the Story of Success* (2008). Through scores of examples Gladwell shows that, more often than not, success results more from deep patterns of social arrangement than it does from individual efforts or merit.

> People don't rise from nothing. We do owe something to parentage and patronage. The people who stand before kings may look like they did it all by themselves. But in fact they are invariably the beneficiaries of hidden advantages and extraordinary opportunities and cultural legacies

> that allow them to learn and work hard and make sense of the world in ways that others cannot.[26]

Taleb and Gladwell argue, so to speak, without benefit of clergy. They hint at, but do not dwell upon, the "self-transcendent" freedom where we come to wonder about our status in the larger scheme of things. What they say appears to reinforce a sense of life as a vast Niebuhrian web of unfathomable intellect, ambition, and impulse, the sort of place where a touch of humility and appreciation of divine grace may not be a bad way to live.

Reclaiming Grace and Mystery

The second volume of Niebuhr's *Nature and Destiny* and the chapters of *Faith and History* put the question of what we can expect in history into a theological perspective. These books ask how, given the vagaries of history, we can live meaningfully over the long haul. As a Christian theologian Niebuhr affirmed that grace-filled existence is joyous existence in the midst of sorrows. Life and history are meaningful because they offer infinite possibilities. Yet history retains its character as nonutopian in a Christian perspective. As the Parable of the Wheat and the Tares (Mt. 13:24–30) suggests, good and evil remain mixed even in the messianic age. "In obvious contradiction to modern liberal interpretations of the power of love in history, Jesus discourages the hope that the preaching of the gospel will banish evil from history."[27] Jesus "rejected every version of the messianic hope which involved God's miraculous intervention in history for the purpose of eliminating moral obscurity."[28] Niebuhr recognized that the quest for eternity is the goal of many philosophies and meditative religions that are less rooted in history. Yet the ambiguity we face in history is not evil; rather a tendency toward evil is more prone to arise "from the fact that men seek to deny or to escape prematurely from the uncertainties of history."[29] If eternity is pursued too consistently on earth, the religious quest removes us from the perplexities of the moral life that matter to Niebuhr's tradition of faith.

Christianity arose within the time-laden historical expectations of biblical religion and Judaism. As a linear tradition it rests on mythic beginnings and endings, Eden and the End of Time, the Alpha and Omega that are celebrated in its iconography. The biblical theme of divine rulership over nature and history shaped Christian perceptions of Jesus of Nazareth as Messiah. Countless theological tracts continue to be written about messianic expectations; they debate the degree to which God's rulership is at hand or lies in the distant, unknowable future. Like most New Testament interpreters, Niebuhr sees that the Alpha and Omega frame the tension-ridden drama of human existence. Accordingly, he dwells on Jesus as a transformer of messianic expectations from the aspiration of national security and unalloyed moral goodness to a path of innocent suffering that unleashed a new way of embracing history.

For Niebuhr the Kingdom of God as a mythic symbol stands beyond human rationality. It stands for an endpoint where the human aspirations for goodness harmoniously meet a beneficent, forgiving Creator God. Without this culture of expectant hope, Jesus would have been unrecognizable as a messianic figure within late Judaism. As a symbol, the resurrection is similarly present and yet future in its unfolding. For Niebuhr the intent of God to create a world ruled by love is clear, even if the divine path to that end remains mysterious, beyond the ken of mortals. History is always in process of realizing the heavenly kingdom on earth; its endpoint lies beyond history in the realm of myth. Yet the imperative to seek justice on earth remains in place, even if humans are incapable of achieving earthly utopias.

Niebuhr sees the fundamental symbols of Christian faith (the Cross and Resurrection) as bestowing meaning on our human endeavors in history. His "eschatology" (reflection about last things) is set forth in these words:

> That the final clue to the mystery of the divine power is found in the suffering love of a man on the Cross is not a proposition which follows logically from the observable facts of history. But there are no observable facts of history which can not be interpreted in its light. When so interpreted the confusions and catastrophes of history may become the source of the renewal of life.[30]

If sin is empirical and validated right before our eyes, the same cannot be claimed for the life of faith. Faith in the foundational Christian message arises, for Niebuhr, not as an answer we have been able to puzzle out for ourselves. Faith arises as a gift and when it does so "there is a consciousness in the heart of the believer that he has been helped to this apprehension."[31] In such an inward religious appropriation "the alternate moods of despair and false hope are overcome and the individual is actually freed to live a life of serenity and creativity."[32] The presence of God in history discloses itself when we least suspect it, always personally and not as the result of intellectual argument.

When we understand how Niebuhr views divine grace working in history, we can also grasp how he came to the view—despite what we might otherwise expect—that "the conflicts of history need not be accepted as normative."[33] The "law of love," which we affirm in our self-transcendence, has a permanent place in the workings of our lives. Even in our broken state, the love of God and our ability to love remain in place. The "foolishness of the Gospel," to use St. Paul's phrase, is unleashed through innocent righteousness and the power of suffering love. The Kingdom of God was at hand in Jesus of Nazareth, though its fulfillment lies in a future beyond the realm of time and history. Not surprisingly, Niebuhr's Christian account of our destiny exudes sober realism about our condition. Chapter 3 of this book makes clear his view that the self-sacrificial love set in motion through Jesus, the supreme moral value, does not easily rule in worldly affairs. As a postulate of political life the pursuit of absolute love on earth can lead to illusory hopes for utopias and new forms of fanatical self-seeking. But the self-giving love of Jesus provides clues on what we can expect and how we are to proceed with our lives in history. If we ask why Niebuhr thinks history is meaningful—despite all its contingencies—his answer rests on the figure of the Christ as delineating the path of history by disclosing a pattern of suffering love that sustains and illumines our existence. By conforming to what the tradition calls "the will of God" our human struggles attain their meaning not through the pursuit of a human ideal, but through a faith in a universal deity that lies beyond human manipulation and wishful thinking.

Even at his Christian depths Niebuhr declined to claim finality for his own theology. He was all too aware that the virtue of his non-Christian friends can exceed that of many Christians. "There is always the possibility that those who do not know the historical revelation may achieve a more genuine repentance and humility than those who do. If this is not kept in mind the Christian faith easily becomes a new vehicle of pride."[34] The Christian symbols that spoke to Niebuhr do not speak to all persons in the same way. Yet they sufficed to assure him that our moral efforts are meaningful. They provided a framework on time and history that lends a sense of divine purpose to our moral endeavors, despite the tragedies of history.

Niebuhr's view of history as full of surprise had the support of the nineteenth-century Danish philosopher Kierkegaard, who viewed history as unfolding freely, full of creative possibilities, even if it sometimes seems like a causal chain. Kierkegaard reflected on the fact that we view the past as closed, the future as open. That view seems sensible enough; the past has in fact already occurred. But what happened already didn't occur because it had to ("of necessity"); we don't hold such a view of our own choices as living persons and moral agents. Kierkegaard struggled to explain why—against appearances—the past isn't more necessary than the future. "To want to predict the future (prophesy) and to want to understand the necessity of the past are altogether identical, and only the prevailing fashion makes the one seem more plausible than the other to a particular generation."[35] The Dane worked hard at getting us to see the mysterious dimension of history. He knew that history was thoroughly unpredictable, full of joyous events and disheartening surprises. This is expressed in Kierkegaard's memorable idea that "life is lived forward, but can only be understood backwards.[36] None of us can predict the actual course of our lives, let alone the larger turns and twists of history. Looking back upon the past, we discover a narrative that more or less accounts for where we have arrived. But how the future will play out is literally seen, in the words of St. Paul, "through a glass darkly."

Secular insight into apparent randomness parallels theological sensitivity toward what Niebuhr considers the final inexpressibility and unknowability of deity. His deity can best be approached through personal confession and heartfelt prayer. Names of God and concepts of God all fall short of the task at hand. If Niebuhr turns to metaphors and symbols, physicists turn to clusters of ideas, like "dark energy." The God of Niebuhr, like the God of John Calvin, does not fit easily into a vest pocket. When functioning at its best religion resists what Niebuhr, following William James, calls our penchant for "lobbying in the courts of the Almighty for special favors." That was his way of emphasizing that authentic prayer ought not to presume to know the full wisdom of God. Similarly, the mysteries of the natural universe also befuddle our ability to figure everything out. Novelist Marilynne Robinson, in a piece called "Credo," says that she is "comfortable with metaphors and analogues from the physical sciences to consider how we think, how we know, how we find our way to places where understanding falters." She continues:

> Knowing nothing about time, I think we mortals may as well assume that we know nothing about causality. At this point we do have enough insight into the fine textures of reality to assume that the primary constituents of reality are, to our minds, exotic in the extreme. Why a human mind, a human life, unfolds as it does, what forces lie behind the historical tides that lift us, strand us, overwhelm us—who can claim to know?[37]

I suspect that Robinson shares the philosopher David Hume's view that beliefs about causality are justified, even when strict knowledge of causal process is lacking. Both are students of the limits of what we securely know. Being aware of our limited knowledge, she thinks, creates an attitude of humility and reverence toward the world. The sentiment is poured out through the words of her clergyman diarist, John Ames, in the novel *Gilead,* "We know nothing about heaven, or very little, and I think Calvin is right to discourage curious speculations on things the Lord has not seen fit to reveal to us."[38]

Niebuhr's sense of history arose from weighing the reading of newspapers and books alongside the biblical perspectives of the Psalms, the prophets of Israel, and the New Testament gospels. His yearlong lecture course on the history of Christian social ethics ran from the New Testament and St. Paul through the seventeenth-century Puritans to modernity and the Christian encounter with other world religions. He knew that Christianity, along with Judaism (Islam was less in his purview) takes the unfolding of history as related to God seriously, a claim that befuddles believers even as it seems implausible to secularists. Niebuhr approached the world with reverence. For him the biblical "love of God" and "love of neighbor" work hand in hand. His faith in a transcendent God of history relates to the incompleteness of our moral choices made on earth.

In approaching Niebuhr it's easy to forget one thing. If God is a way of naming the supreme mystery of the universe—as is surely the case for Niebuhr—the human as a perplexed moral agent is only slightly less mysterious. Niebuhr's lifework suggests that he had enough on his hands pondering the human self. Unlike the stereotype of a theologian, he is not interested in angels, the hereafter, or splitting hairs over arcane points of religious doctrine. He has no particular use for the "divine proofs" of philosophers. As Niebuhr once put it in a 1926 sermon on "the Foolishness of Preaching": "No one can be lifted into the presence of God by a syllogism."[39] Theology and ethics are, for him, not matters of speculation. As intellectual pursuits, they are thoroughly earthbound, tied to the moral perplexities and self-doubts of our lives on a daily basis.

In the end, the task of coping with our anxiety as we face the future is more personal than intellectual. Niebuhr's sense of hope rests on the assurance of faith that—right now, not just in the distant future—a merciful God finds us to be acceptable. Since it's so easy for us to fall short of the mark, having a penitent heart is the mark of true religious faith. Niebuhr's sense that history unfolds through suffering love breaks with the apocalyptic strands of the tradition that project either cataclysmic Doom or a beatific Eden (or mixtures of both) at end of time. His sense of unfolding divine purpose rests on a faith, as John Adams stated in writing to Jefferson, that I can "rejoice in God and his creation and exult in my own existence." After citing this in a sermon, Niebuhr wryly observed that Adams's phrase sounds somewhat heretical. Yet the Psalmist, he is quick to remind us, made a similarly joyful confession: "I am fearfully and wonderfully made: marvelous are thy works; and that my soul knoweth right well" (Ps 139:14).[40] In the Christian faith meaning and fulfillment are found both in the present moments of our lives and in our future hopes. The power of fulfilling love, though still incomplete, is found in the opportunities that history provides for continued renewal and new beginnings.

3

RECOGNIZING HUMAN AMBIGUITY

Niebuhr's concept of original sin solved certain problems for my generation. The 20th century was, as Isaiah Berlin said, 'the most terrible century in Western history.' The belief in human perfectibility had not prepared us for Hitler and Stalin. The death camps and the gulags proved that men were capable of infinite depravity. The heart of man is obviously not O.K.

Arthur Schlesinger, Jr., "Forgetting Reinhold Niebuhr," *New York Times,* September 18, 2005

Niebuhr's thought is complex, but he is properly known as the theologian of conflicted humility—for his belief that human nature is flawed and fallible even, or especially, in the pursuit of good causes.

Michael Gerson, "The Irony of Obama," *Washington Post,* October 22, 2008

I consider original sin both radically compassionate and, as doctrines go, fairly verifiable.

Marilynne Robinson, author of *Gilead* and *Home,* in "Credo," *Harvard Divinity Bulletin* (Spring 2008)

Let me state it bluntly: Niebuhr believed that humanity is afflicted with excessive pride and a self-preoccupation that distorts moral judgment. For him this view was an empirical fact of human experience, borne out in everyday observations of human affairs. He pondered long and hard on the question at hand. A thoroughly modern man widely read in Christian theology, Niebuhr understood the reality he observed in light of the teaching of original sin. He knew that the term "original sin" did not sit well with many of his contemporaries. But it was the stubborn, often sordid, reality of the human condition that caught his attention. His way of coming to grips with it was shaped by a prolonged debate with the ways that Christianity understood and explained the highs and lows of human existence.

Niebuhr's account of "the grandeur and the misery of man" (Pascal's phrase) has always received more attention during times of crisis. That is why we are again reading him today. He achieved prominence in the generation that wrestled with the moral consequences of the Holocaust and first use of the atomic bomb. Faced with such moral depravity and the potential for annihilation of modern civilization, Niebuhr felt compelled to probe for answers. When, soon after World War II, a troubled Niebuhr was depicted on the cover of *Time* magazine, March 8, 1948, his picture was accompanied with the heading: "Man's story is not a success story." Even a mass magazine recognized the possibility that profound disarray lurks within human endeavor.

By all reports Reinhold Niebuhr was especially good at the task of thinking about human nature. It's the key to grasping what is distinctive about his thought. Niebuhr didn't invent this way of thinking, but he gave it his own stamp. He did so in awareness that Christian teaching about human sinfulness is often despised and little understood, even by Christians who are regular churchgoers. Some persons leap to the conclusion that Niebuhr secularized the doctrine of sin. How otherwise could he have so many admirers among atheists and agnostics? To my mind, at least, that response is premature. It's not so much that Niebuhr secularized but that he humanized the age-old Christian teaching. Since religion is thought to point beyond the world of everyday experience, the task of giving a human face to doctrinal teachings may initially seem odd. In Christian antiquity Augustine also sought to make Christian teachings square with our experience in the phenomenal, everyday world where we live. Like Socrates, Augustine brought divine truth down from heaven and applied it to our human quandaries.

The interest in Niebuhr among political writers often touches lightly upon his teaching regarding sin. Selective appropriations of his thought are more the order of the day. He is represented as a deep thinker with a knack for allowing moral suspicion to illumine events of the day. It is no easy task to ferret out the lineage in biblical religion and Christian social-ethical teachings that informs Niebuhr as a thoroughly modern man. The background of his thought is not on display on every page that he wrote.

The present chapter aims at tracing Niebuhr's teaching on sin to its sources in Christian tradition and raises questions about how an apparently outmoded religious way of viewing our condition can be a living option for Niebuhr and possibly for our contemporaries. We've already seen that Niebuhr recognized the potential oddity of his stance when he wrote in 1932 that "the effort to combine political radicalism with a more classical and historical interpretation of religion will strike the modern mind as bizarre and capricious."[1] However bizarre this may be, there's no getting around the fact that permutations of the traditional Christian doctrine of sin loom large for Niebuhr.

St. Paul, Augustine, and Kierkegaard

In *Nature and Destiny* and elsewhere Niebuhr drew from a Christian understanding of human nature that was introduced, refined, and sustained in the teachings of St. Paul, Augustine, the Protestant Reformers, and Søren Kierkegaard. Like John Calvin, Niebuhr was impressed by the pronouncement of St. Paul that "all have sinned and come short of the glory of God" (Romans 3:23). The first book of his Gifford Lectures shows the human as more duplicitous and ambiguous than suggested by classical antiquity and by much of the modern post-Enlightenment world of Europe and America. Niebuhr was not concerned to deny that we consist of both mind and body. Yet he wanted to emphasize that we are defined more as agents, makers, and doers with intentions than we are as minds or as bodies. This view has ramifications for how we understand ourselves in relation to religion and politics. As a student of history Niebuhr drew from a long tradition of reflection on human nature in order to confront the foibles, hopes, disappointments, and hidden ironies that persist in our modern era.

Early in mid-career Niebuhr encountered the teaching of Augustine from the late fourth to early fifth century. He never departed from having discovered this ancient Christian writer of such remarkable substance.[2] Like Augustine, Niebuhr saw that our minds are intimately associated with a will that can stand tall and noble or succumb to what we desire, want, and love. As Eric Gregory puts it in a major study of Augustinian ethics in modernity: "Human beings are bundles of loves."[3] More than his Platonic predecessors, Augustine was aware of the fickleness and fragility of the will, its easy ability to follow a disordered desire. Both Augustine and Niebuhr see human history as a "mixed picture" where love of self contends with the love of God (substitute, if you so wish, any universal value greater than oneself). Augustine puts the matter memorably in *The Confessions,* book X.28: "In adversity I long for prosperity, in prosperity I fear adversity. What middle place is there between these two when the life of man is not all trial?" There is no "middle place" or steady human state for Augustine. The same holds for Niebuhr. When things go well, I immediately fear that this will end. When I face adversity I immediately long for better times, a favorable turn of fortune. In fact, the instability and restlessness of the human is a lesson that can probably be gleaned by simple honesty and self-examination. But knowing that a major writer has eloquently expressed such a view helps us see the depth of the idea and its potential relevance for us today. That's one of the benefits of having a sense of history.

In addition to reading Augustine and the Bible, Niebuhr was reading the philosopher Søren Kierkegaard (1813–1855) in German in the late 1930s, before the Danish writer had been translated into English. If we wonder why Niebuhr seems relevant in a new time of troubles, it's partly because, along with Kierkegaard, he had discovered "the remarkable self-destruction of individuality in modern culture,"[4] through the superficiality of the social and political masks that we wear. Writing in the mid-nineteenth century, Kierkegaard famously saw the dangers in the herd thinking of modernity. He anticipated that the media would create a phantom called "the public" and sway the crowd through public opinion. In his day, the analysis was based entirely upon newspapers and satirical literary rags. Kierkegaard's *Two Ages: The Age of Revolution and the Present Age* (1846) reads like a primer on the ability of mass (today we would say media-driven) society to run roughshod over the needs of individuals, when life seems like an endless series of committee meetings, surrounded by idle chatter.

> By this chattering the distinction between what is private and what is public is nullified in a private-public garrulousness, which is just about what the public is. For the public is public opinion that is interested in what is utterly private. Something that no one would dare present at a meeting, something that no one would be able to speak about, something that even gossips would scarcely admit to having chattered about, can very well be put in writing for the public. . . .[5]

In continuing his analysis Kierkegaard treats the dynamics and effects of existing anonymously in a mass society where the individual person becomes lost in a media circus called "The Public." In such a situation we feel helpless and excluded, like outsiders and spectators, and "it all finally ends with the whole age becoming a committee."[6] Kierkegaard's further analysis of human despair in *Sickness unto Death* agrees with Augustine that the self consists of immense instability, the reality of which we can scarcely ever admit to ourselves.[7] We long for a state of equilibrium, a measure of happiness that is steady and reliable. But there's no equilibrium at hand. If we are willing to face ourselves honestly, we see that life as a steady state isn't exactly on offer.

We've looked at the elements of human nature as Niebuhr understands them, the fact that we consist of mind, body, and will. For Niebuhr, like Augustine, the human will is central to our intellectual makeup; acts of thought are invariably accompanied by aims and intentions. The Augustinian view points to a dynamic but unstable human self, full of tension between our desires and fears of bad outcomes of these desires. Niebuhr appropriated Augustine's richly interior sense of self in *The Confessions,* which maintains that we are a mystery unto ourselves. The Augustinian self is restlessly driven by anxiety about the future. Our habit of continually weighing the events and persons around us on a moral scale complicates matters further. As thinking creatures with wants, loves, and desires, we constantly attach moral value (positively or negatively) to our aims and to the pursuits of others. We quickly identify fraud when we see it, even if we are the last to sense its presence in our own lives. It's easier to lament our situation or decry the peculiarities of other people who do not share our sense of self, our family values, or the ways of our nation.

Niebuhr knew that St. Augustine is widely considered anathema for his teaching on the Christian doctrine of sin and he did not uncritically take over an inherited piece of Christian teaching. Augustine took the fall of Adam literally and imagined that the original act of sin in the Garden of Eden was perpetuated to the human race through the sexual act. In contrast, Niebuhr consistently takes "the fall of Adam" symbolically, not literally. Adam is everyman, more than the human story's original villain. As a modern Augustinian Niebuhr emphasizes Augustine's view of sin as a form of pride. In his *Confessions* Augustine views sin more flexibly, not just associated with the misuse of the body, as if our bodies and sexuality are evil. Sin arises in acts of inflated pride (*superbia*), or even more powerfully as strong desire (*concupiscentia*). Augustine uses the Pauline language "sins of the flesh" as well as "sins of the eyes." But he doesn't think of these as restricted to the delights of what we do with our bodies or see with our eyes. Rather, for Augustine, the phrase "sins of the flesh" (using the language of St. Paul) points to the multiple ways that a disordered desire for power is enacted in our lives. We may misuse our bodies or those of others sexually; but we may also misuse the physical labor of others by unfair labor practices. Similarly, we may sin with our minds through the arrogance of our knowledge, as when we lord it over others with our intelligence or put them in their place through the unconscious arrogance of social class and inherited privilege.

If Niebuhr sees strong-minded persons yielding to the sin of pride, he's equally aware that less confident individuals often commit the sin of sloth or laziness where we take refuge in immediate distractions and sensual pleasures to avoid reaching for higher goals or ideals. *Nature and Destiny* speaks of this "sin as sensuality" as more widely noticed and socially condemned than pride because "it is a more apparent and discernible form of anarchy than selfishness."[8] Where pride reaches beyond the center of the human self among persons of ambition, sloth tends to be content with the habits and impulses within our reach that give us pleasure. This second form of sin is less often observed in Niebuhr's thought, since he spends so much effort combating the sins of the powerful. But his inclusion of sloth as sinful is significant. Its antidote lies in our being willing to take moral risks and act with a sense of social responsibility in human affairs.[9]

What Niebuhr finds significant in Augustine, a full-blown Christian account of our humanity, did not begin with the fourth-century saint. Our potential for duplicity is reflected in the sayings of Jesus of Nazareth with their relentless critique of hypocrisy and in St. Paul, who astutely records a set of interior musings and puzzlements. Many, if not most, of Jesus's parables are concerned with the duplicity of the human heart. Far from being harmless moralizing stories or allegories, the parables of Jesus are weapons of controversy, inducements to new self-awareness that, in the words of John Dominic Crossan, "give God room."[10] St. Paul expressed something similar in his letter to the Romans, chapter 7, where he famously puzzles over the problem of a conflicted self-awareness: "For I do not do the good that I want, but the evil that I do not want is what I do" (Romans 7:19). The singular Pauline insight into the conflicted human self divides Niebuhr's teaching from the forms of confident rationalism that we typically associate with modern culture.

We may think that St. Paul is extreme, that it is quite possible to see what is good or right and to pursue morally sound actions. In fact, Paul doesn't deny that possibility. It's just that the Pauline insight comes into play during those self-reflective moments when we realize that our deeds or thoughts differ from our own moral ideals. Niebuhr thus takes from Paul the sense that we are something of a puzzle, even to ourselves. At the same time, it's important to note that, for Paul, the human isn't simply evil. We have knowledge of morality and the fact that this knowledge is "holy, right, and good" (Romans 7:12). The trick is that a discrepancy so often obtains between this moral knowledge and what we actually do. When this happens, it reveals inner self-doubt and moral confusion.

Since the impetus for my actions is not transparent, I am a mystery even to myself. Self-evaluation is suspect, biased by wishful thinking and denial. I'm never in a position to be the best judge of my own behavior. New Testament parables as well as the dialogues of Socrates show how difficult it is to give up the presumption of knowledge, especially of being in the right intellectually and morally. There is a universal tendency to overestimate one's virtue, to have a relatively easy conscience and think that I have truly earned or merited all the good things that have ever happened in my life.

Even more than the ancients (or at least on a broader scale) we believe in education and pride ourselves on intelligence. Ancient Greek philosophers could not entertain the idea that we might know the good, as they put it, and not do or enact that which we know. Like the ancient Greeks, we believe we are rational animals. Yet for thinkers like Paul, Augustine, or Niebuhr, our rationality is not the whole story.[11] Uses of the mind are as potentially fickle as the uses of the body. Being smart may get us into trouble, especially when we're overconfident of the virtue of our intelligence. The distinction between being intelligent and being wise consists of having an ability to learn the lessons of the past and having a sense of one's limits. Ambition and self-certitude are wiser, more tolerable and useful, when they are (at least partly) chastened. As *New York Times* writer Frank Rich reminds us, the title of David Halberstam's 1972 book on John F. Kennedy's team, *The Best and the Brightest,* was meant to be ironic. It identifies the confident moral hubris that led to the Vietnam War. Halberstam knows "the difference between intelligence and wisdom, between the abstract quickness and verbal facility which the team exuded, and true wisdom, which is the product of hard-won, often bitter experience."[12]

Power Has Consequences

In addition to the features of the human self just sketched, Niebuhr's picture of the human requires us to see how the tendency to pride and self-preoccupation relates to relationships of power. Understanding Niebuhr on power is a first step toward grasping how his concern for justice relates to the Christian ideal of self-giving love. Having looked at elements of our nature (will, in addition to mind and body), it is crucial for us to see the analysis of power in his thought. Awareness of the incongruities of power relationships and imbalances of social hierarchies came to Niebuhr through the Bible with its prophetic sense of justice and through Karl Marx with his acute critique of capitalism. Analyzing not just sin but the consequences of sin that arise within diverse relationships of power marks the distinctive contribution of Niebuhr to Christian social, political, and economic thought.

In *Moral Man and Immoral Society,* Niebuhr writes that our proclivity to perpetuate sin is greater in institutions and groups than among individuals. We are even less moral in groups and nations than we are as individuals.

> Individual men may be moral in the sense that they are able to consider interests other than their own. . .. But all these achievements are more difficult, if not impossible, for human societies and social groups. In every human group there is less reason to guide and to check impulse, less capacity for self-transcendence, less ability to comprehend the needs of others and therefore more unrestrained egoism than the individuals, who compose the group, reveal in their personal relationships.[13]

Individuals are freer in their ability to self-correct and admit mistakes, while self-interest and survival are the norms of our collective life. However that idea may seem today, it dropped like a bomb on theological liberals in the 1930s.[14] The core insight stands as a signature belief, even if by 1965 Niebuhr playfully accepts that the 1932 title might better have read: "The Not So Moral Man in His Less Moral Communities."[15] In fact, the reformulation is more accurate. Niebuhr's earlier thought never attributes moral purity to individuals or denies that generosity of spirit and compassion can arise within groups. It's just more difficult for groups, and especially nations, to break into acts of generosity and forgiveness than it is for individuals.[16] The political thrust, including that of economic and political power, is ever present in his thought.

In addition to the view that sin is more difficult and pervasive within groups than it is in individuals Niebuhr holds that the consequences of sin are greater when committed by the powerful. *Nature and Destiny* speaks of this in a section called "the equality of sin and the inequality of guilt." At first the phrase seems like word play. But the reality it expresses rings true to events in the present, not just in some distant Christian-influenced past. The double-edged proposition states that (a) the tendency toward sin (pride or sloth resulting in moral blindness) is universal in humans, and (b) the effects of sin are experienced differently, depending upon our stations in life and the preexisting cards we have been dealt. Like Dante in the "Inferno," Niebuhr distinguishes between levels of culpability.[17] In their hidden, devastating ripple effects fraud and betrayal in high places can outrank an act of murder. The consequences of sin done by people with power and influence are far greater than the consequences of sin among people with less social clout. The tradition behind this draws from a sense of social solidarity that goes back as far as Aristotle and includes the biblical sense of being a people for whom the deeds of one affect all. In doing wrong as well as in doing what is right, none of us stand alone. Our deeds are enacted in the context of the earth and other human lives.

In contrast with Niebuhr, much of modern liberal as well as evangelical Protestantism is haunted by individualism, the quest for successful lives as individuals. Where that concern dominates, social engagement with the world suffers. Although Niebuhr admires the trenchant analyses of the human self in need of divine grace of Luther and Kierkegaard, he thinks both figures underestimate the social dimension of religion and its power. Like him, they operate out of a classical Christian "two kingdoms" theory. But Luther and Kierkegaard are more "dualist" than Niebuhr in distinguishing and protecting the spiritual Kingdom of God (to use time-honored theological language) from the sordidness of worldly affairs. By contrast, Niebuhr's teaching consists of a "mixed reality" that less securely states the divide between good and evil, whether in individuals or among groups. Niebuhr's Christian social ethics, his main field of teaching, is more activist than Luther or Kierkegaard. He sees that the selfless love of the New Testament love commandment must square off with the demand to do justice if we are to hope for proximate (even if not perfect) solutions in the realm of politics. Having a prideful and self-preoccupied human heart doesn't lessen the moral imperative to do good in the world.

Love and the Struggle for Justice

As a seminary professor, Niebuhr taught in the fields of social ethics and applied Christianity. It was his job to teach future pastors and preachers to make abstract ideas—God's love, the meaning of Jesus Christ, judging and forgiving human folly—connect with life in the world. We've seen how *Moral Man and Immoral Society* addresses power relations in the social order. That book also expresses Niebuhr's contention that the nonviolent resistance of Gandhi is coercive, even if it doesn't actively use force.

> While [Gandhi] confuses the moral connotations of non-resistance and non-violent resistance, he never commits himself to pure nonresistance. He is politically too realistic to believe in its efficacy.[18]

Active in the pacifist Fellowship of Reconciliation out of revulsion from the slaughter in the trenches of the First World War, Niebuhr had broken with pacifism by 1932. That same year he called for protest against the Japanese invasion of Manchuria, an event that foreshadows his 1940 call for America's Christians to give up isolationism and pacifism to enter the struggle against Fascism.[19] (We'll see that his turn from pacifism remains a sore point for some of his Christian critics). As a teacher of social ethics, Niebuhr had wrestled with the Social Gospel movement and believed that its liberalism tried to eradicate evil without having an adequate social strategy.

His 1935 title *An Interpretation of Christian Ethics* states Niebuhr's difference with the Social Gospel movement of Walter Rauschenbusch as "making a sharper distinction between love and justice."[20] Although Niebuhr's later thought added more subtlety and nuance, the book is a vigorous read on the problem of "how it is possible to derive a social ethic from the absolute ethic of the gospels." In contrast with the Gospel ethic, he writes:

> A social ethic must be concerned with the establishment of tolerable harmonies in life. . . . All this must be done, not by asking selfish people to love one another, neither by taking their self-love for granted. These harmonies must be created under 'conditions of sin.'[21]

A chapter of this book, "The Relevance of an Impossible Ethical Ideal," describes Jesus's absolute commandment to love one another as "an impossible possibility," when applied to issues of war, peace, economic and social justice. The paradoxical formulation conveys the reality as well as the perils of selfless love. Self-sacrificing love is in principle "possible," for we humans are angels as well as brutes; but pursuing selfless love is "impossible," since angelic virtue cannot readily achieve its ends amid a selfish ("fallen") world. To be sure, acts of altruism occur within troubled families and among heroes in war, situations of conflict where the self is forgotten for the sake of someone else. Such moral deeds constitute the highest ethic of all, the standard that grounds all morality, including justice, which of necessity works on a different plane. Even mutual or shared love between two or more persons rests initially on some aspect of self-giving love. Otherwise the risk of initiating relationships of mutual love would never have been undertaken.

Although he later criticized the early book,[22] Niebuhr never deviated from the view that we cannot run the world, a school, a business, a nation, or even a church organization, on the purely self-sacrificial love taught by Jesus. (Even within family life, our most organic place of loving relationships, psychologists often speak about a need for tough love.) Yet the lofty "turn the other cheek" ethic of Jesus remains in place, a permanent reminder of the highest form of love.

Reflecting on love led Niebuhr to expound on the distinction between love and justice as conflicting moral ideals. Perfect equality is de facto an absurdity among humans, owing to the fact that we differ in age, sex, intellectual and other abilities, including social and genetic backgrounds. It's impossible to reconcile the inspiring power of forgiveness with the calculating requirements of justice. Turning the other cheek is a recipe for disaster as a matter of public policy, even if the teaching of Jesus delineates the moral standard by which we measure our deeds.

> Jesus is suggesting in his Sermon on the Mount that you cannot be moral if you are too strictly moral. . . . Nobody who is strictly moral can forgive, because forgiveness is at once the fulfillment of every concept of justice, and its annulment.[23]

Love requires the coercive power of justice to secure the gains of idealism. Love can be verbally espoused more easily than justice can be achieved. But the affairs of the world can never be conducted solely on the principle of love.

At the same time, justice can never be achieved based upon some quid pro quo of perfect equality. Preexisting social and economic arrangements don't allow it. The requisite calculations rest on incommensurable, even unknowable, factors. Unlike empirical objects and measurable behaviors, goodness cannot be quantified.[24] There is no Dow Jones average for assessing the ebb and flow of morality. If there were, we'd see immediately how slippery the moral life has become.

Jesus's New Testament parable of the "Workers in the Vineyard" (Matthew 20: 1–16) makes this point. In the parable's plot a series of workers are hired and the first hired agree to work for a daily wage. Four more groups of workers arrive every few hours, and at the end of the day, all are paid the same, though only the first group had agreed to that wage. When the initial hirees grumble against the landowner that the last ones who got the same payment only worked for an hour, while they labored all day in the hot sun, the landowner responds: "Are you envious because I am generous?"[25] The good master appears to overpay those hired later in the day, while keeping the contract with the first hired. As Niebuhr sees the oddly provocative little tale, "the divine mercy is challenged for being unjust and defended because it exceeds justice."[26] It looks like a bad way to run a business; but then that isn't what the parable is really about. In the end, calculation of any kind is at odds with the pure agape (Greek for self-denying love) ethic of Jesus.

Before leaving the topic, I need to clarify two points regarding the implications of Niebuhr's teaching on love and justice, forgiveness and judgment. First, it's necessary to recognize that the imperative to do good and to struggle for social justice remains fully in place. It's a mistake to take away from Niebuhr the view, "Why try, since we ourselves and the world around us are so corrupt." For him, it's in our nature to try; the sense of moral good runs through our being. We are not evil per se, just sinners, and they are not the same. The divine imperative to be moral, to love God and our neighbor, remains wholly in place. To paraphrase St. Paul in Romans: There is no excuse, despite the dire prognosis. Living in a fallen world provides no license to slack off or become morally complacent.

> Frequently, believing Christians are tempted by their recognition of the sinfulness of human existence to disavow their own responsibility for a tolerable justice in the world's affairs. Justice is not love. Justice presupposes the conflict of life with life and seeks to mitigate it. Every relative justice therefore stands under the judgment of the law of love, but it is also an approximation of it.[27]

The impetus to work for justice remains constant in Niebuhr. A powerful example of this is documented in David L. Chappell's *A Stone of Hope: Prophetic Religion and the Death of Jim Crow* (2004) on how the ideas of prophetic religion led the civil rights movement of Martin Luther King. While repeatedly noting Niebuhr's influence, Chappell reminds us that King's doctrine of man is "practically identical with Niebuhr's."[28]

Second, a platitude of Western thought that refuses to die, even though it's patently false, is that the Old Testament exclusively teaches a God of judgment, while the New Testament does the same for a God of love. In truth, both testaments of the Bible teach God as loving redeemer as well as judge of human affairs (Psalm 136's refrain, "for his steadfast love endures forever" and Romans 1:18, "The wrath of God is revealed from heaven against all ungodliness and wickedness"). Like many stereotypes, this one seems to draw from a (slightly different) kernel of truth; representations of deity in the Hebrew Bible become more transcendent and universal (less tribal or national) as biblical history proceeds. The idea of the New

Testament as morally superior to the Hebrew Bible persists. In the long history of problematic relations between Christians and Jews this idea is utterly pernicious. The phrase "the angry God of the Old Testament" crops up in all walks of life as a truism, among literature professors, psychologists, scientists, atheists, and Christian clergy. It belongs to the religious illiteracy that clings to the Christian faith and its permutations in the wider culture. Niebuhr's thought is (literally) unthinkable for anyone who clings to the stereotype.

The Semantics of Sin

It's ironic that Niebuhr's teaching on sin, which brilliantly explains American imperialism to political writers, is so widely shunned by liberal and progressive Christians. Aversion to the classical Christian doctrine of sin makes renewed interest in Niebuhr a theological nonstarter in some quarters. Since it first came under fire in the eighteenth-century Enlightenment, "sin" has increasingly slipped from view in the Western world. The Age of Reason called for humans to be their best and gave birth to the idea of progress; yet Niebuhr is a critic of the idea of human perfectibility, a hallmark of Enlightenment teaching. For him, the depths of human perversion, deception of self and others, is endemic. In what he called "our technic society" of bourgeois capitalism it is as apt to occur within religious institutions as within economic and political institutions.

Among present-day Christians confessions of sin are largely confined to conservative evangelicals and to the liturgical celebrations of Catholics, Lutherans, Presbyterians, and Episcopalians. Sin is anathema to most liberal and progressive Christian groups, whether the megachurch movement, classical Quakers, humanists, and secular scientists. As historians of theology know, the liturgies, creeds, and teachings of Eastern Orthodoxy (Greek, Russian, Syrian, or Armenian) do not dwell as much on sin as do the traditions of the Western church (Roman Catholic and Protestant churches of the sixteenth-century Reformation).[29] No comparable doctrine exists in classical or in modern Judaism. Rabbinical interpreters of the Adam and Eve narrative (Genesis, chapter 3) see good and evil impulses (*yezer ha-tov,* and *yezer ha-ra*) as equally present possibilities in each moment of our existence. Niebuhr's friend, Abraham Heschel, held the traditional Talmudic view that there were always thirty-six unknown righteous "by whose merit the world survived."[30] Unlike Western Christianity,

Judaism has no permanent tilt toward falling short of the mark. Early Christianity evolved out of dire times of crisis within late Judaism, including the Roman destruction of the Jewish Temple in 70 C.E. The idea of "Adam's fall" with universal consequences for humanity entered the theological lexicon in St. Paul's Letter to the Romans, chapter 5. The doctrine that arose in the religious-political crises of late antiquity and was brought to prominence through St. Paul was then given classical shape in the theology of Augustine.

In our day, however, the fate of sin is more precarious than I have indicated. Sin may even be viewed on a par with the medieval crusades as an extreme aspect of Christianity that has done more harm than good in the world and should now be left behind. If the crusades embody violence directed outward, sin as an account of God's judgment is perceived as a form of personal violation. Mentioning "sinful humanity" or "confessions of sin" is met with indifference, if not scorn. The phrases remind hearers of hellfire, damnation, and the guilty conscience of a misfired religious upbringing. It is little wonder that one continually meets persons within liberal religious circles who describe themselves as recovering Lutherans or recovering Catholics who seek psychological relief from religion-induced, guilt-ridden lives.

Much of the Christian world has turned against, or at least modified, the ancient doctrine of sin. Thomas Cranmer's sixteenth-century Prayer of General Confession from the Church of England's Book of Common Prayer captures the mood of the classical confession. This version of the prayer book was most familiar to Niebuhr, who occasionally worshipped in the Episcopal tradition with his wife, Ursula Niebuhr.[31]

> ALMIGHTY and most merciful Father; We have erred, and strayed from thy ways like lost sheep. We have followed too much the devices and desires of our own hearts. We have offended against thy holy laws. We have left undone those things which we ought to have done; And we have done those things which we ought not to have done; And there is no health in us. But thou, O Lord, have mercy upon us, miserable offenders. Spare thou those, O God, who confess their faults. Restore thou those who are penitent; According to thy promises declared unto mankind In Christ Jesus our Lord. And grant, O most merciful Father, for his sake; That we may hereafter live a godly, righteous, and sober life, To the glory of thy holy Name. Amen.

There's little doubt that the Book of Common Prayer captures Niebuhr's realism regarding the tragic, but redeemable, human condition. Today, however, the despised phrases, "there is no health in us" and "miserable offenders" are perceived as groveling and have been excised from most Christian prayer books, even when similar sentiments remain in place.[32] Defenders of the phrase "there is no health in us" point out that the offending words, which are in the plural, make a claim about our general spiritual-moral condition "in the eyes of God." The words simply acknowledge prayerfully that there is no easy moral equilibrium in our lives, however much we might wish that this were not the case. Theologians remind us that the Creator God as Judge and Redeemer sets standards in the light of which humans universally fall short of the mark. Sin is, after all, described in classical Christianity as rebellion against God, the ground and source of true moral order.

Today the traditional language of sin is thought to be psychologically damaging. Reciting such prayers is viewed as unhealthy, undermining a sense of self-worth and self-esteem. The popular psychoanalyst, Erich Fromm, author of *The Art of Loving* and a refugee from Hitler's Germany, "felt there was a certain satisfaction in [Niebuhr] at the evilness of man, rationalized in theological and philosophical terms."[33] When his 1978 best seller, *The Road Less Traveled,* equates sin with laziness, M. Scott Peck implies that with hard work sin/laziness can be overcome.[34] The practice of confession has fallen into disuse in many U.S. Catholic churches. Post–Vatican II liberal Catholics generally seek to take positive, progressive political positions, even if the bishops and hierarchy urge otherwise. The very figure of Augustine, so central to Niebuhr's imagination, is singled out as especially villainous. Within Roman Catholicism in the 1980s an anti-Augustinian movement around (former monastic) Matthew Fox contrasted the term "original sin" with "original blessing" to affirm the fundamental goodness of his fellow human beings. Best-selling titles by scholars of the early church move in a similar direction. Elaine Pagels's popular book *Adam, Eve, and the Serpent* (1987) decries the Augustinian teaching of original sin as if it were the hallmark of a deviant tradition within Christian thought.[35] Yet a revisionist account of Christian doctrine cannot obscure the dominance of sin and grace as signposts of the Western Christian tradition.

Apart from conservative evangelical Christians and mainstream liturgical traditions, other Protestant Christian writers shy away from talk about sin. A search of the magazine *Sojourners* and its founder Jim Wallis's books, *God's Politics* (2005) and *The Great Awakening* (2008), confirms this for the popular movement of progressive, socially engaged evangelical Christianity.[36] The pages of *Sojourners* speak with conviction about the oppression of the poor, care of the earth, the evils of war, and need for economic justice.

Appealing to evangelicals to care for the earth is part of the specific call to repentance of this movement. Clearly some things have gone very wrong in the world being addressed by Jim Wallis. Wallis's books are full of uplifting admonitions to do good works, to mobilize on behalf of the poor, and otherwise pursue the work of the Gospel message. But the author of the best-selling *God's Politics* rarely speaks of the human condition as sinful.

Other champions of liberal or what is today called progressive Protestant Christianity try to avoid direct mention of sin but keep its reality. In *The Heart of Christianity* (2003) Marcus Borg acknowledges that some things have gone seriously wrong with humanity. He notes that humanity losing its way is the storyline of the Bible. But Borg wishes to drop the term "sin," which has too much negative baggage. Instead he thinks we can describe the reality of "being lost" by using multiple metaphors. Another popular writer, Bishop John Shelby Spong, in *A New Christianity for a New World* (2001), employs a similar strategy in a chapter called "Original Sin Is Out; The Reality of Evil is In."[37] Such writers wish to drop the word, but (somehow) keep the reality of sinful humanity in place. By redescribing human folly in diverse ways, Borg and Spong give up the power and elegance of a universal explanation of the human condition. Their books are helpful to many searching Christians, but they don't speak to the issues of politics addressed by Niebuhr. Liberal minds, as we're aware, like pluralism and interpret Jesus and the Bible today with less attention to the larger Christian tradition. This approach leaves the field clear for other wholesale explanations of the human that are currently on offer, including the rival account of a Christian feel-good optimism that fails to do justice to the fragile and stubborn aspects of human nature.

The battle over the semantics of sin will scarcely be settled by what I write here. At a time when Niebuhr's account of self-preoccupied human nature rings true to political pundits and opinion-makers, Americans by and large remain hostile to this aspect of his teaching. They see it as psychologically and morally debilitating and remain indifferent, believing that it plays no role in their lives. Perhaps it is just a matter of semantics; the word "sin" may have too many misleading connotations. But I suspect that it's the underlying hard teaching about the human condition, which cuts against America's residual idealism, to which Americans object. In the era of rampant financial deceptions that serve the greed of capitalist entrepreneurs, the fundamentals of Niebuhr's position still illumine contemporary life. It's little wonder that Niebuhr believed that everyday experience of the world confirms the Christian doctrine of original sin.

Hopeful Realism

We've seen that Niebuhr's understanding of human nature as sinful arises from a reading of the Christian past that also posits something distinctive about the Christian understanding of history. Against some popular depictions of Niebuhr, he is not a theologian of doom and gloom. His message calls us to live meaningfully in the present with hopes for the future.[38] The previous chapter ended with a sketch ("Reclaiming Grace and Mystery") of the grounds for faith and hope in his theology. The task of living with expectations in history is never completed; if things were otherwise, there would be no need for human hope. Stated in Christian language: the courage that enables us to have moral aspirations rests upon the discovery that elements of grace and forgiveness are at work alongside our natural impulses and prudential calculations. Along with St. Paul and Augustine, Niebuhr never wavered from viewing love as the law of life, even if it is imperfectly embodied in our historical existence.

It bears repeating that viewing our nature as sinful does not make us evil in some pure and simple sense. There's no need for Christians to deviate from Aristotle's view that "man is by nature a rational animal." That seems obviously true and commonsensical; among all living creatures humans are distinguished by a high sense of rationality. Niebuhr believes that we are characterized by a magnificent capacity for rational thought. That's the glory and grandeur of the human race. Yet, as I've observed in these pages, human rationality also operates in conjunction with will and thus with the devious interests of the self.

I previously cited Marcus Borg's suggestion that it's time to substitute multiple metaphors for human shortcomings and drop the use of the term "sin." Perhaps that idea has merit. In his late publication, *Man's Nature and His Communities,* Niebuhr considers a similar alternative, apparently for some of the same reasons.[39] But in noting that he made a "pedagogical" mistake in speaking about "original sin," Niebuhr still thinks of the doctrine as symbolically and historically correct. He appears not to have acted on his self-doubt, and it is probably good that he didn't. In Borg's liberal progressive Protestantism our human dilemmas are approached less prescriptively. In the name of pluralism a variety of ways of describing humanity might be used, perhaps on alternate Sundays. Or many ways might be combined in a new declaration: "Sin and forgiveness would become only one way that we talk about our problem."[40] What is lost in Borg's proposal is the universal element that occurs in all human beings: the ways that pride and moral blindness distort our sense of self and make us believe that we are more virtuous than is the case.

Sin is a tough sell in modernity. Since it can't be measured, those who are committed to crunching numbers as the requisite path to truth will remain unimpressed. But as long as self-righteousness persists among humanity, something like the classical notion of sin (in the sense of Augustine and Niebuhr) remains cogent. As a "hard teaching" of the Christian tradition, it resists being watered down through an appeal to liberal instincts. Niebuhr helps us explain how individuals and nations can step over the bounds and get into radical moral disarray. Like all good theories, a compromised theory loses its explanatory power. It also yields fewer occasions for self-examination or for thinking about tragic aspects of the human story and of how we might best confront them.

I've noted that the cover story of *Time* magazine in March 1948 picturing Niebuhr ran as its subhead: "Man's story is not a happy story." Niebuhr was critical of the view that happiness as self-contentedness can ever be the goal of human existence. Learning to live as a fallible mortal, learning to live while aware of one's ignorance and limits, is closer to the path of Jesus of Nazareth. It is also closer to Socrates and to what is required for the global human community to flourish in dangerous times. In his day Niebuhr stood as the antithesis of Norman Vincent Peale's "power of positive thinking." A similar injunction to positive thinking and optimism has grown and assumed new forms among contemporary Americans. If believers and skeptics are stunned by his dogged insistence upon human sinfulness, this may be a sign that Niebuhr's analysis connects. His view has the advantage of enabling us to pursue our moral aspirations based on an account of the world as it is, not as we might wish it to be.

4

CONNECTING WITH WIT AND WORDS

Reinhold Niebuhr is not famed as easy reading, but is at times a study in precision as when he says, "The self does not realize itself most fully when self-realization is its conscious aim. . . ."

Poet Marianne Moore, from the 1958 essay "Idiosyncrasy and Technique," in *The Complete Prose of Marianne Moore,* ed. Patricia C. Willis (New York: Viking, 1986)

Hawk-faced Reinhold Niebuhr, one of the most respected of U.S. theologians, is a strenuous man. When he lectures, his arms jab and flail the air; when he talks to friends he often changes his seat or walks about puffing cigarets [sic]; he is not content to pour out ideas about God & man; he wants to make them work in the imperfect world of political action. Yet his reiterated text is man's powerlessness to act for his own salvation.*

** Left-of-center Dr. Niebuhr is staff contributor to the Nation, chairman of the militantly liberal Union for Democratic Action, a pressure group of intellectuals and union leaders, which maintains a Washington lobby, publishes a bi-weekly commentary called Congressional Newsletter.*

Time magazine (January 6, 1947)

We've seen how Niebuhr's awareness of human ambiguity and fallibility speaks to global economic and political crises. His sense of history contributes depth to that perspective. It allows him to draw from distant examples to illumine events of the present day. His large number of published books and articles show an uncanny ability to assess the teachings of modern as well as pre-modern texts, secular as well as biblical and theological. Like many writers, Niebuhr was a voracious reader and book reviewer. Anyone wishing to chronicle his times can read the nearly 140 reviews, editorials, or articles he did for the *Nation* alone between 1920 and 1950. They touch upon work by (or about) a list of cultural notables that includes Crane Brinton, Barrington Moore, Jr., Arthur Koestler, Allan W. Watts, Perry Miller, Jonathan Edwards, Geoffrey Barraclough, Karl Jaspers, Winston Churchill,

Jacob Burckhardt, Archibald MacLeish, Sidney Hook, Edmund Wilson, Lewis Mumford, John Dewey, and Thomas Mann. Alongside teaching Christian social ethics at Union Theological Seminary, Niebuhr pursued an alternative curriculum of his own making.

It's difficult to imagine any writer more engaged with his times, let alone a man of the cloth. The case of Thomas Mann, the leading novelist and a refugee from Hitler's Germany, is instructive. It provides a glimpse of the patrician literary figure's high regard for Niebuhr. In Germany Mann had written *Reflections of a Nonpolitical Man* (1919) in defense of an aesthetic world of letters unsullied by politics. With the terrible rise of Nazism and flight to America Mann reversed direction, gave speeches, and wrote essays on behalf of democracy and the war effort. Niebuhr's *Nation* review of Mann's *Order of the Day: Political Essays and Speeches of Two Decades* (1942) notes, among other wry touches, that the volume "does handsome penance for his previously avowed indifference to politics." In a four-page typed letter, mostly in German, Mann responded to the theologian's review. He says he reads the *Nation* in part because Niebuhr contributes to it and thanks him for the attentiveness bestowed upon his book. Although Mann had not yet seen others, he imagines the review is "the most significant and deeply penetrating, which has been written about it."[1]

Niebuhr's reading tastes were broad and eclectic. His interests in literature and poetry were representative of his era. But the depth of insight he carried with him invariably informs the pages of his published works. There's a benefit to browsing through cultural history with Niebuhr. When he weighs lessons of the past, his words speak to the present. His sense of cultural memory has an uncanny ability to cull and to probe philosophical and literary positions with an eye to how they shed light on the present. He draws not only from specific historical events but also from literary and philosophical monuments that reflect struggles in other times and places. Too little attention has been given to Niebuhr as writer, an author whose work glitters with characteristic turns of phrase, themes, and interests. A vociferous polemicist and Christian apologist, Niebuhr as pulpit orator and political provocateur weighs and compares the worldly wisdom that surrounds him with moral insight gleaned from the Christian faith. We do well to pause, halfway through this book, to ponder the religious and secular sources of Niebuhr's insight, his appropriation of classical and modern texts, while asking how these sources fed his imagination.

We typically don't give much thought to how philosophers or theologians use language to connect with an audience. Exceptions to that are, of course, Nietzsche in philosophy and Kierkegaard in theology, both brilliant stylists and writers. Theologians are not generally known for the quality of their written expression. But that has not always been the case. The most effusive man of words of ancient Christianity, St. Augustine, combined rich rhetorical expression with logical investigation. Thomas Aquinas was a formalist par excellence and worked within a tight grid of systematic questions. More logical than rhetorical, Thomas to this day appeals to trained philosophical minds. Luther was a man of effective communication, a remarkable biblical translator, and a powerful voice that came close to single-handedly launching the sixteenth-century Reformation. In turn, his French counterpart John Calvin, trained in humanistic learning of his day, was a superb French and Latin stylist. Arguably the most brilliant penman among major philosopher-theologians was the nineteenth-century Dane, Søren Kierkegaard. His way of combining literary and religious-philosophical perspectives still confounds his interpreters. His invention of dramatic masks (pseudonyms) to express much of his thought appeals to us through its individualized perspectives. Philosophers are relatively inept at assessing Kierkegaard's use of irony, which says one thing but means another and thus seems like lying. For similar reasons tidy minds sometimes have difficulty with the paradoxical ideas of Niebuhr.

This chapter asks what makes Niebuhr, the essayist, preacher, and writer of theological and political prose, so memorable. What are the secrets of his appeal? Like other political realists, Niebuhr is a writer of prose. He is neither a poet nor a dramatist. Writing the 1948 Niebuhr cover story for *Time* magazine, then senior editor Whittaker Chambers describes the style in this way, "The twists & turns of his reasoning and his wary qualifications are not hedging, but the effort to clamber after truth. He knows that simplicity is often merely the misleading coherence of complexity."[2] Niebuhr's expressive formulations combine words in ways that speak to hidden dimensions of the problems we face as political, economic, and, at least for some of us, religious animals. His epigrams and aphorisms readily pop up if we take the trouble to search out Niebuhr quotations, either online or in print. In his hands double-edged sayings are deployed not for their own sake—to be admired as clever—but to illumine the dilemmas of human existence.

Like the Self, Words Are Complex

As preacher in university chapels, Niebuhr spoke to believers, skeptics, seekers, and lost souls. Although he was no poet, Niebuhr had unnerving insight into the vagaries of the human heart. If the British playwright, the late Harold Pinter, is said to have had a "gift for finding the ominous in the everyday,"[3] it could be said that Reinhold Niebuhr had a gift for finding the ominous in our good intentions. Like the eminent playwright, Niebuhr knew that language conceals as much as it reveals. Becoming aware of what we conceal when we are morally conflicted defines the task of self-understanding. Whether he was preaching or writing books and essays, Niebuhr used wit and irony to make us aware of our problems and predicament. He was talented at connecting head and heart as well as relating time-honored religious teaching about sin and grace to the rival worldviews of the social-political marketplace.

It's surprising, for some even disconcerting, to find felicitous expression in a writer of theological texts. Niebuhr's emphasis was on substance more than aesthetics. But his ability to reach an audience of religious and secular readers drew from rhetorical gifts and literary sensitivity. He had a feel for the poetic rhythms and elements that cling to religion in its classical forms. The Protestant Christianity of his German forebears was exceptionally verbal. Luther's masterful 1534 translation of scripture shaped high German culture.[4] We forget that the Psalms of ancient Israel, a constant source of Niebuhr's insight, are written in metrical, though not rhyming, verse. It's easy to fall into the trap of viewing history as facts and poetry as a less practical, even an effete, art form. In Niebuhr's writing both history and poetry are grist for a deeper understanding of life's contradictions.

Niebuhr's feeling for the cadences of the spoken word echoes the Psalms and the Episcopal Book of Common Prayer, while relating these insights to modern life. *The Irony of American History* illustrates how a sense of history combines with theology to espouse the age-old Christian virtues of faith, hope, and love (1 Corinthians 13). In mid-page we confront the words:

> Nothing that is worth doing can be achieved in our lifetime; therefore we must be saved by hope. Nothing which is true or beautiful or good makes complete sense in any immediate context of history; therefore we must be saved by faith. Nothing we do, however virtuous, can be accomplished alone; therefore we are saved by love. No virtuous act is quite as virtuous from the standpoint of our friend or foe as it is from our standpoint. Therefore we must be saved by the final form of love which is forgiveness.[5]

Citing this passage in a review of the reissued book, David Bromwich comments that Niebuhr's "prose sometimes rises to an intensity that is close to prayer. . . . No italics mark the place, but most readers of the book will certainly pause here."[6] The oft-quoted passage makes four points: Our mortality limits human accomplishments; all that is good participates in the transiency of history; human achievement requires a social-communal world; and we are never as virtuous in the eyes of others as we are in our own. The Christian virtues of hope, faith, love, and the heightened form of love called forgiveness are given political relevance, not as absolutes, but to embolden his readers. Included in a chapter that criticizes the American assumption of a link between "Prosperity and Virtue," Niebuhr reminds us that self-proclaimed moral achievement is illusory and suspect. Rather than preach the Pauline virtues of faith, hope, and love, Niebuhr gives them new life by infusing our sense of mortality with moral obligation.

In Niebuhr's hands the pendulum constantly swings between secular issues of the day and the insight of biblical tradition. The 1944 title *Children of Light and Children of Darkness* presents his theory of democratic politics at a time when a war-weary America still sought victory over Germany and Japan. It invites readers into a conversation in which biblical thought is deftly interwoven with political philosophy and moral wisdom. In warning about the perils of democracy, not just for a newly constituted Germany, Niebuhr writes: "Man's capacity for justice makes democracy possible, but man's inclination to injustice makes it necessary." The aphorism captures the duality of the human condition. It honors secular wisdom for its shrewdness. The book's title alludes to the New Testament parable of the Dishonest Steward (Luke 16:1–13), where Jesus of Nazareth, the implied master in the story, favors the cleverness of a knave over more timid souls. Verse 8 of the parable states that "the children of this world are wiser in their generation than the children of light." In Niebuhr's hands the "children of light" are the foolish and vain idealists, while the "children of darkness" are cunning and despairing cynics. Though cynics invariably defeat idealists, the idealists will act more prudently if they know this. Secular experience thus confirms the Bible's realism, even as a biblical turn of phrase sheds light on our collective ambitions, fears, and moral shortcomings.

It is not just the distant poetry of the Bible and religious liturgy that impressed Niebuhr. He had significant contact with living poets and writers. Lionel and Diana Trilling were part of the Niebuhrs' intellectual circle.[7] After moving from England to New York in 1939, the poet W. H. Auden (d. 1973) became a lifelong friend, especially of Ursula Niebuhr.

Auden's biographer, Edward Mendelson, notes, "During the next few years, most of Auden's political and ethical positions were indistinguishable from Niebuhr's."[8] Auden published in Niebuhr's journal *Christianity and Society,* and both did book reviews for the *Nation.* The distinguished American poet Marianne Moore (1887–1972) began to admire Niebuhr in the late 1930s, saw him as one of a "few men of Socratic wisdom among us," and recommended his sermons and writings to literary friends Ezra Pound and Elizabeth Bishop. A 1952 congratulatory letter upon publication of *The Irony of American History* applauds the work for containing "certain axioms rivaling scripture."[9] Moore, who hailed from a notable Presbyterian family, cites the phrases, "Nothing however virtuous can be accomplished alone" and "even the best human actions have some guilt." Moore avidly read the Niebuhrian "house organ" *Christianity and Crisis,* became a family friend, and attended some of Niebuhr's classes in the 1950s.[10]

It would go too far to maintain that Niebuhr is a poet. But he drew parallels from poetry and cultural history to show how biblical and theological wisdom shed light on the quandaries of personal and political existence. He read poetry deeply, committed some of it to memory, and understood its affinity with religion. Poetry traffics in particulars and details, generalizing from specific moments of experience. Poet Stephen Dunn reminds us why poetry is needed to illumine the nooks and crannies of our minds.

> Most of the language used in a day, I would say, maybe about 75 percent of it, is designed to deceive you. . . . I think one thing poetry does is bring us a little closer to the real by the precision of its language. To get the world right is a hard-won thing. It's not easily done."[11]

The quirks of subjective awareness arise from contingency and surprise, often when we least suspect it. "History repeats itself, but never in the same way" fits the pattern, as does Niebuhr's belief that "sin is inevitable, but it isn't necessary." Some things are bound to occur, but they happen freely, unexpectedly, and we're only half-aware of the process. Paradox and irony mirror the complexities of our existence. Like a poet-prophet, Niebuhr was in the business of finding words that connect and did so with apparent ease.

Niebuhr's literary preferences were eclectic. They were drawn from a wide spectrum. Literary allusions that range from the Victorians to Shakespeare's Hamlet and the Psalms dot his sermons. Niebuhr cites English poetry as well as the nineteenth-century American writers, Emerson, Whitman, and Melville. The highly intellectual modernist poetry of Pound, Eliot, or Stevens is not evident in his work. Lines from Robert Browning's poem on the human life cycle, Rabbi Ben Esra, turn up in *Leaves from the Notebook of a Tamed Cynic* (1929) and in *Beyond Tragedy* (1937). His sermons draw from the early twentieth-century Illinois "prairie poet" Vachel Lindsay. They also use lines from Stephen Vincent Benet, Henry van Dyke, the Victorian Matthew Arnold, and the *Rubaiyat* of Omar Khayyim, both to illustrate points positively and to pinpoint human folly. His work cites the English World War I chaplain, Geoffrey Studdert-Kennedy, who stood in the trenches of the dying and subsequently became the greatest pacifist in Britain.[12] Rudyard Kipling's poetry expresses for Niebuhr the fond hope of fulfilling universal human aspirations, while Elizabeth Barrett Browning's words convey a facile longing for tranquility. Studdert-Kennedy, Kipling, and Browning pop up in the 1946 collection of sermons, *Discerning the Signs of the Times*. In contrast with such writers' idealistic aspirations, the sermons teach us to look at life with sober suspicion, even as we seek to be, and to do, our best as humans.

Religious Language as Poetic

In a splendid little book called *Hopeful Realism: Reclaiming the Poetry of Theology* (1999), Douglas F. Ottati calls for a renewal of the poetic sources of the Christian tradition.[13] The language of sermons, hymns, and prayers, Ottati maintains, has a power to break through the chatter and humdrum reality of everyday life. Although the book draws much from H. Richard Niebuhr, its analysis also fits his brother. We've seen how Reinhold Niebuhr distrusts the way modernity appeals to our nature as rational animals. For all of its practical benefits, prudential reason cannot address the riddles of our existence as effectively as the language of religion. Commenting on the banalities and sentimentalities of the average Protestant worship service, he writes that

> religion is poetry. The truth in the poetry is vivified by adequate poetic symbols and is therefore more convincing than the poor prose with which the average preacher must attempt to grasp the ineffable.[14]

His communicative skill was honed in the pulpit and on the political and university podiums. He appreciated the beauty and drama of liturgy and the dignity of devotion. But he didn't aspire to edify through beautiful oration. In the diary from his Detroit parish he notes: "I will never aspire to be a preacher of pretty sermons. I'll keep them rough just to escape the temptation of degenerating into an elocutionist."[15] The self-musings continue:

> I wonder whether there is any way of being potent oratorically without over-simplifying truth. . . . Every artist does, after all, obscure some details in order to present others in bolder relief. The religious rhetorician has a right to count himself among, and take his standards from, the artists rather than the scientists. The trouble is that he is usually no better than a cartoonist.[16]

Niebuhr was suspicious of religion as mere edification, apart from moral sensibility. His interest in the quirks of humanity accords with Nathaniel Hawthorne in *The House of Seven Gables:* "What is called poetic insight is the gift of discerning, in this sphere of strangely mingled elements, the beauty and the majesty which are compelled to assume a garb so sordid."[17] His prose invites us to wrestle with conflicting ideals (self-love versus love of others; loyalty to family versus loyalty to the larger human community) that defy formulaic resolution. He was a master at portraying the disturbing antinomies between love and justice, nature and history, human pride and our sense of the good, self-reflection and social activism.

Looking back on Niebuhr we can discern a complex grasp of the need of religious language to be paradoxical, to express the contradictions of our existence. Sermonic essays "As Deceivers, Yet True" (1937), "Mystery and Meaning" (1946), and "Coherence, Incoherence, and the Christian Faith" (1953) make clear that the language of religion—to be authentic—must hew a line that respects the final mystery of life without succumbing to the magic of superstition or to the illusion that our knowing minds have fully unraveled the secrets of the universe. In 1927 he wrote in his ministerial diary that

> one half of the world seems to believe that every poetic symbol with which religion must deal is an exact definition of a concrete or an historical fact; the other half, having learned that this is not the case, can come to no other conclusion but that all religion is based upon fantasy.[18]

Like St. Paul in his admonitions in the Second Letter to the Corinthians (2 Cor. 6:4–10), Niebuhr espouses a view of life that embraces oppositions: living while dying, being joyful amid sorrow, being poor while making many rich. What seems true at one level is deceptive at another. "For what is true in the Christian religion can only be expressed in symbols which contain a certain degree of provisional and superficial deception."[19] What all this means can be clarified if we ask what light basic Christian creedal formulations throw on our understanding of life.

By hindsight it's instructive to see how Niebuhr wrestled with the closing words of the Apostle's Creed, "I believe in the forgiveness of sins, the resurrection of the body and the life everlasting." At the time of his ordination to ministry, his reaction was not unlike that of many persons today who espouse the tradition but are suspicious of supernaturalism.

> We were not certain that we could honestly express our faith in such a formula. If we were finally prevailed upon to do so, it was usually with a patronising air toward the Christian past, with which we desired to express a sense of unity even if the price was the suppression of our moral and theological scruples over its inadequate rendering of the Christian faith.[20]

But a quarter of a century later Niebuhr had come to see that belief in the resurrection of the body "expresses the whole genius of the Christian faith." He explains:

> The idea of the resurrection of the body can of course not be literally true. But neither is any other idea of fulfilment literally true. All of them use symbols of our present existence to express conceptions of a completion of life which transcends our present existence.

His act of claiming or owning "bodily resurrection" affirms the view of a human self as physical as well as mental. The article of faith attempts to express the Augustinian view that the body as such is not evil and that the created order is good. To his mind the article of faith has little to do with a resuscitated corpse. He views creeds as poetry become petrified and thinks they mean most when sung and celebrated, not pronounced as rigid dogma. The act of avowing a creed affirms a truth of religious poetry rendered into prose.

In a similar endorsement of the Apostle's Creed, contemporary novelist Marilynne Robinson speaks about its opening words, "I believe in God the Father almighty, Maker of Heaven and Earth." For her, the words rescue earth "from the ancient opprobrium of dualism, the notion that creation was the work of an evil god, a demiurge, and is itself evil." For the novelist the creeds

> do not proscribe other beliefs or enforce behaviors as evidence of orthodoxy, but instead implicitly define orthodoxy as the affirming of essential elements of sacred narrative, briefly interpreted.[21]

It may not be accidental that Robinson, like the theologian Niebuhr, holds to a sense of the creed's underlying affirmations. Both seem to be driving at the open-ended and unfinished nature of human existence in a world larger than our ability to give literal answers. Scientific thought can only take us so far in meeting this legitimate need. For Niebuhr the processes of nature and of history are not wholly "self-derived or self-explanatory." He thinks that final explanations of the universe must rest content with an image or likeness, that is, symbols that represent the origination and the sustaining energy of the universe. For Niebuhr being aware of the limits of knowledge leads to reverence and humility in our striving to understand the ends of life on earth, including the life of politics, culture, and moral aspiration. Like artists who use distortion to convey a proper sense of perspective, Christianity uses symbol and metaphor to convey some sense of the presence and power of a realm of mystery that lies within, but also beyond, the causal chain.

The Pulpit as Nontrivial

If Niebuhr were an armchair theologian, we would not need to touch on his work in the Protestant pulpit, a task he took to be central to his calling. His sermons, and his approach to giving them, tell us a great deal about the interior life and calling of Niebuhr as a Christian. What they reveal supplements and helps complete our sense of Niebuhr as polemicist and political writer. Niebuhr managed not to be dull as he railed against the triviality of modern preaching with its moralizing admonitions. It was pointless to preach that the world would be better if we were only more loving. In his sermons the King James cadences of the Psalmist and St. Paul mingle with criticism of the triviality and conventionality of the churches. A favorite Niebuhr phrase from the Psalms speaks to the moral temptations of modernity: "But as for me, my feet were almost gone; my steps had well nigh slipped. For I was envious at the foolish, when I saw the prosperity of the wicked" (Ps. 73:2–3).

Two collections of edited and reworked sermons were published in his lifetime, *Beyond Tragedy* (1937) and *Discerning the Signs of the Times* (1946). His wife, Ursula Niebuhr, issued a third volume, *Justice and Mercy* (1974), which prints additional sermons, along with his prayers. To this, the diary of his Detroit pastorate, *Leaves from the Notebook of a Tamed Cynic* (1934), adds musings from his early ministerial formation. Niebuhr pursued his profession as a preacher for more than fifty years, and he preferred it to teaching.

> After a quarter of a century in academic life, I can still understand why I was so reluctant to leave the local parish. Academic life seems highly

specialized in comparison with the life of a parish priest meeting human problems on all levels of weal and woe, and trying to be helpful in fashioning a 'community of grace' in the barren anonymity of a large city.[22]

During decades of crisis-ridden American life he spoke in college and university chapels across the nation, thus becoming known to scores of students. Thinking about him as a leader of public worship brings us closer to the subjective and pastoral side of a public figure.

Niebuhr knew that the role and task of a preacher in our society was daunting. Ministry required the skill of a generalist who must do without the professional safeguards of well-understood expertise. In the year he was called to Union Theological Seminary (1928) he wrote that ministry requires

> the knowledge of a social scientist and the insight and imagination of a poet, the executive talents of a business man and the mental discipline of a philosopher. . . . Our task is not specific enough to make a high degree of skill possible or to result in tangible and easily measured results.[23]

Doing the work of ministry is daunting, to say the least. "To speak the truth in love is a difficult, and sometimes an almost impossible, achievement. . . . I'm not surprised that most budding prophets are tamed in time to become harmless parish priests." But for a strong-minded figure like Niebuhr, the challenge of being ruthlessly honest with individual persons in their dealings with worldly affairs made the church the most exhilarating place to be.

Niebuhr came from a strong preaching tradition. He grew up in the German Reformed Church, which became the Evangelical and Reformed Church (1934) and merged with Congregationalists to form the United Church of Christ in 1957. Like Paul Tillich and Wilhelm Pauck, Niebuhr preferred the undogmatic orientation of this denomination. In New York he typically worshipped at the Seminary's nondenominational James Chapel and during the last decade of his life he worshipped at the Congregational Church near the family's summer home in Heath, Massachusetts. His Protestant Union roots in northern Germany stood in a tradition that honored both Luther and Calvin, hence put the task of preaching front and center. But he had misgivings about the centrality of the sermon within the Protestant churches, at times viewing it as a lost art form within the Christian faith. Compared to Catholic or Anglican worship he viewed his own tradition as quasi-liturgical, using a mix of form and freedom in its services.

Writing about "The Weakness of Common Worship in American Protestantism" (1951), Niebuhr asserts that prayers should contain biblical material and phraseology in a way that mediates between past and present. "If this is done to excess the relevance of the Biblical faith to contemporary experience may be obscured. If it is not done at all the contemporary experience is not transfigured by the Biblical insight."[24] The standard is well met in the prayers that Niebuhr wrote for use in worship. In such prayers deeply personal petitions ("Help us to live in the trials of our day with patience and to meet our tasks with courage") are set alongside concerns for the political world ("Look with mercy upon the peoples of the world, so full both of pride and confusion, so sure of their righteousness and so deeply involved in unrighteousness, so confident of their power and so imprisoned by their fears of each other").[25]

In the sixteenth century Luther had equipped Protestant worship with a lectionary—a yearly cycle of scriptural texts—so that a minister would not just preach on hobby topics or, as Luther put it, "on blue ducks."[26] Triviality in the pulpit is not authentic to the classical Reformation or to Niebuhr. The sheer banality of popular Protestantism—including the inability of liberal religion to address sinful humanity—troubled Niebuhr. With Luther he held that "living and dying make the theologian" not just trying to be a cheerleader for Christ or assuaging consciences by the platitude that we're surrounded by God's love.

A glance at sermon titles in the collection *Justice and Mercy* ("We See Through a Glass Darkly," "Law, Conscience, and Grace," "Beware of Covetousness," "Be Not Anxious," "The Son of Man Must Suffer") bears out Niebuhr's view that a proper Christian sermon must be "an invitation to self-analysis."[27] This book's final chapter returns to the theme of self-awareness in the teaching of Jesus and Socrates. To initiate that task, a sermon should be designed to awaken the conscience from complacency, while instilling realistic hope that may lead to renewal. Niebuhr's life experience taught him that nontrivial preaching confronts human injustice, while awakening the possibility of a change of heart. Like his Protestant forebear, Martin Luther, he knew that the process of repentance and a change of heart leads to our having a sense of divine grace and forgiveness. On Niebuhr's view, awakening of a need for repentance lies at the moral depth of our existence. The process differs greatly from merely admonishing people to be good or seeking special favors from the deity.

Between Tragedy and Stoicism

As we've seen, Niebuhr views human life as ambiguous and the tendency toward prideful acts and deeds as inevitable though undertaken freely. We typically describe ourselves as optimists or pessimists and will doubtless continue to do so. Yet neither word does justice to Niebuhr, even if his account of the human condition has overtones of tragedy and he is most critical of the wishful thinking of optimism. That was the basis of his assault on the Wilsonian idealism that he had initially espoused; it is also why moral revulsion over the 2003 Iraq War has brought him new readers. Niebuhr is suspicious of the belief of contemporary political science that more accurate surveys and quantitative data are tools that will improve human destiny. Like the journalist Robert D. Kaplan, he found the political and literary classics to be superior to conventional political science in plumbing the disorders and disasters of history. Quantitative analyses of modern social and political science do not shed light on sheer altruism or on gratuitous evil, the extremes of human behavior. Descriptive statistical data may confirm or disconfirm trends and expectations. But they offer little wisdom regarding individual and collective moral struggles. Such wisdom is more apt to arise from classical texts that treat politics than from the "value free" work of social science. As Kaplan, a veteran overseas journalist for a quarter of a century said in *Warrior Politics,* "It was the shock of seeing wars, political upheaval, and Third World poverty firsthand that drew me to the classics of philosophy and politics, in the hope of finding explanations for the terrors before my eyes."[28] A return to Thucydides, Livy, Machiavelli, and Kant provided Kaplan with fresh perspective.

Niebuhr drew similarly from philosophical and literary classics. He frequently touched upon two such strands of thought, ancient Greek tragedy (especially Aeschylus and Sophocles) and Roman Stoicism (Epictetus and Marcus Aurelius). Looking at them helps us grasp how his distinctive theological position relates to these traditions. Doing so helps us see how his view of humanity embraces elements of "pessimism" and "optimism," while it resists a simple use of such labels. In popular usage the epithets "tragic" and "stoic" resonate in American discourse. By staking out humanity's place in the cosmos tragedy and stoicism deal with the religious themes of life and death. Unlike the popular optimism of American culture, tragedy and stoicism confront the fact of evil in the world and the human need to cope with its reality. For both suffering is real and not apt to disappear, even with our best efforts. Each teaches something noble in its view of how we might live less hubristically. To Niebuhr tragedy and stoicism consist of elements that resemble, but are not the same as, the picture of humanity that he takes from the Christian faith.

Let's take them up in turn. A sermon, "Christianity and Tragedy," in the collection *Beyond Tragedy* explores similarities and differences. Niebuhr speaks of tragedy in the following way. When we use the word "tragic" for horrible events that might, or might not, have been prevented, we react with sorrow. There is nothing noble or uplifting in acts of murder or in the snuffing out of a child by a drunk driver. Most deaths (whether from disease, accidents, or wars) are unheroic. We are apt to react with a mixture of pity and compassion and say that such events are tragic. Yet ancient Greek tragedy, like Christianity, stands between pure pessimism and optimism. It appeals to something noble in the human spirit, where human vitality rises up to challenge, and eventually succumb to, the laws of the gods. The "tragic hero" undergoes suffering and death in order to uphold the good. "He suffers because he is strong and not because he is weak. He involves himself in guilt not by his vice but by his virtue."[29] If we have tears, they are the tears of an admiring spectator.

The model of Jesus willingly dying on the cross resembles tragedy, at least superficially. In this case, as in tragedy, death is also taken on for a greater good. But that isn't the whole story. In Niebuhr's sermon text, Luke 23:27–29, Jesus says to the daughters of Jerusalem, who are aware of his fate: "Weep not for me; but weep for yourselves and for your children." Whereas a Greek chorus urges us to weep for the tragic hero, Jesus tells his followers to "weep for themselves." The difference, Niebuhr argues, is that in Christianity the reaction is not one of spectators only, but of participants who are freely involved in the sin and guilt that kills the hero. Through the act of weeping for oneself, one enters into the healing posture of repentance. If the defect lies in a distorted human goodness and not in life itself, there is room for hope. This is not fate or destiny, but a new possibility.

The ancient Greeks dealt with this enigma by celebrating the struggle between humans and the fate decreed by the gods. Christian faith has more in common with Greek tragedy than either has with the optimism and prudential rationalism that reign supreme in much of modernity. But compared to Greek tragedy Christian faith looks more deeply into our subjectivity, the universality of our foibles, and our consequent guilt. For Niebuhr, repentance, the theological word for acknowledging we've fallen short of the mark, takes the first step toward moral healing and a new sense of well-being.

If Greek tragedy marks one aspect of comparison with Niebuhr, ancient Stoic teaching marks another. Here again, in popular usage "stoic" describes any act of living through suffering with courage. If tragedy flirts with pessimism, stoicism flirts with optimism. No matter how difficult, things will turn out all right in the end. As a personal attitude and philosophy, strands of Stoicism run just beneath the surface of Western thought.[30] Its teachings are famously enshrined in a book of meditations that record the inner life of the second-century Roman Emperor Marcus Aurelius. It surprises when a public figure can find philosophic repose while acting at the pinnacle of worldly affairs. The late Secretary General of the United Nations Dag Hammerskjöld's book *Markings* provides a parallel example.[31] Elements of Stoicism sometimes remind readers of aspects of Buddhism. No appeal is made to a personal deity; rather, a divine element (Greek: the *Logos,* reason or word) runs through the cosmos and is accessible within human consciousness. Although Stoicism was an ancient Greek school, the texts of Stoics that we have derive from ancient Rome and consist of work by Seneca and Epictetus, in addition to Marcus Aurelius.

Some of Niebuhr's critics see a Stoic sensitivity running through his quest for serenity amid life's troubles. Niebuhr concentrates on the self-awareness of humans more than on the age-old doctrines of Christ, the Trinity, and the hereafter espoused by the tradition. An element of Calvinism in Niebuhr regarding the overarching power of deity may reinforce an impression of a divine determinism to which humans must invariably submit. The prominent British theologian, John Milbank, believes Niebuhr is a Stoic who masks his true position with Christian language.[32] (The issue returns in a section of chapter 6.) In fact, Niebuhr does seem like a Stoic in one respect. He shares the Stoics' sense of a deity that is all-encompassing and ever present in the universe in which we live. There's a large realm of "the given" in Niebuhr's thought. Humans are not their own makers or the makers of the universe, and we live best when we act in light of this fact. Like Rainer Maria Rilke and the Psalmist, Niebuhr knows that we do not own the universe. Phrases from the Psalms attest to the human as creature, not Creator, and answer the question of who owns the earth in the words, "The earth is the Lord's and the fullness thereof . . ." (Ps. 24:1). Similarly, though the poet Rilke is more a religious seeker than a Christian writer, his *Book of Hours,* "Do not be troubled, God, though they say 'mine' of all things that permit it patiently," chides the human tendency to act as if we own and thus seek to control, all that we touch.[33]

Those are the positive resonances between Niebuhr and Stoicism. His stance seems close to the Stoic advice of Epictetus, a first-century contemporary of St. Paul, to "fully accept what you cannot control." But a close reading of Niebuhr will not equate his view with Stoicism. He is at pains not to endorse the Stoics' emotional indifference (*apathea:* apathy) and utter submission to (divine) cosmic law. These points become clear if we take a glance at Niebuhr's famous Serenity Prayer.

> God, give us grace to accept with serenity the things that cannot be changed, courage to change the things that should be changed, and the wisdom to distinguish the one from the other.[34]

Aligning Niebuhr with Stoicism would be more plausible if he had ended the prayer with its first injunction: "To accept with serenity the things that cannot be changed." For Epictetus, all the things that cannot be controlled are external to mind; hence, one's attitude is the primary focus. The first-century philosopher holds that, like a favorite teacup that may break, if we treat a wife and children as mortal, this makes it easier to bear their loss.[35] That may be sagacious in the abstract. But the example illustrates a moral and emotional indifference that is antithetical to Niebuhr. It flies in the face of the biblical commandment not just to love God, but to love the neighbor. The peace of mind of the Stoics, Niebuhr says, is "not the peace of a real self, but of a mind detached from the self."[36]

Niebuhr is less cut and dried than Epictetus about how we know what is under our control. Given Niebuhr's account of human ambiguity, this should occasion no surprise. His realism invites us to worry about and pray over the issue of what lies beyond our control. Where Stoicism is matter of fact, the "Serenity Prayer," adopted and adapted for use in the recovery programs of Alcoholics Anonymous, suggests that there's need for grace even in our deciding what is within or beyond our control. Niebuhr sees the self as more dynamic and less intellectualistic than do the classical Stoics. He's more attuned to human vulnerability and the fickleness of the human will when caught between the moral imperative to do good and the temptations of power and self-aggrandizement.

A Contextual Thinker

Niebuhr was no ivory tower academic. Typically he wrote on and about specific occasions, prompted by the threat of global war or nuclear destruction, the outbreak of violence in the labor movement, or the struggle for racial equality under the law. A bold thinker, he was against the pretension of grand schemes as a matter of principle. This is forgotten when professional theologians fault Niebuhr for not giving a tight exposition of the full round of Christian theology. We've repeatedly noted that his interest lies in practical Christian teaching, not in theory. (His biographers Richard Wightman Fox, Charles C. Brown, and Ronald H. Stone give the details of his multifaceted engagements with political and religious institutions of American and international life.) There is a pragmatic dimension to Niebuhr. He was consistently in favor of getting things done, taking some kind of action to advance the cause of justice.

For Niebuhr truth is in the details of life. In a way his stance as writer doesn't need further explanation. Most of us are generalists in meeting the tasks of life—not experts. Even here Niebuhr as a contextual thinker also has intellectual parallels. In explaining his play *Galileo,* Berthold Brecht famously espoused the view that "the man who does not know the truth expresses himself in lofty, general, and imprecise terms."[37] Through specific words and deeds dramatic art deflates our natural smugness.

Deflating intellectual pretension was also a pastime of the early nineteenth-century German Romantics, Friedrich and August Wilhelm Schlegel, and their theological friend, Friedrich Schleiermacher. Niebuhr would certainly have resisted, if not rejected, this resemblance. He consistently uses the term Romanticism with negative connotations. He knew that later political Romanticism had unleashed destructive nationalism and fostered grandiose views of Germany that eventually led to Adolf Hitler. Niebuhr was suspicious of Thoreau and Whitman for thinking there is a "peace of nature that man can claim as his own and be redeemed by."[38] But the early German Romantics epitomized contextual thinking and used it consistently to explore human subjectivity within political community. Niebuhr's approach as a writer resembles the insight of early German Romantics that rational systems of thought can never catch up with the unfolding mystery of the universe. Friedrich Schlegel, for example, preferred literature to philosophy. His collection of aphorisms undercut formal philosophy by writing that "novels are the Socratic dialogues of our time."[39] Among today's reading public Schlegel has certainly won the day. Serious readers, keenly interested in the perplexities and contradictions of life, are more apt to seek solace and courage in novels than in philosophy. Yet philosophy and theology are needed as much as ever in today's world, even if their abstract claims occasionally run roughshod over the particularities of lived experience.

For his part, Niebuhr was always ready to burst the bubble of professorial abstractions and of specialized views of the world that mistake expertise for wisdom. Like his counterparts among the early Romantics, Niebuhr disturbed smug certitude by addressing the quirks in our lives and our beliefs. To encounter his thought afresh is to be made aware of one's own complacent habits of mind. His assault on self-satisfaction applies to religious minds as well as to their atheistic and agnostic critics.

5

REVISITING AMERICA WITH IRONY

The most eerily timely [article] may be an essay written more than seventy-five years ago: Reinhold Niebuhr's, on America's struggles as an imperialist power.

James Fallows, national correspondent for the *Atlantic,* commenting on the occasion of the magazine's 150th anniversary, July/August 2006 on Niebuhr's piece "Awkward Imperialist" from May 1930

The times in which we live call for a Niebuhrian revival. To read Reinhold Niebuhr today is to avail oneself of a prophetic voice, speaking from the past about the past, but offering truths of enormous relevance to the present.

Andrew J. Bacevich, Professor of International Relations and History, Boston University, "Introduction," to Reinhold Niebuhr, *The Irony of American History* , University of Chicago Press, 2008

Thus far we have looked at major aspects of Niebuhr's thought, how he thinks about history, the unfolding drama of the human condition, and his work as writer and preacher. Like a hedgehog, he burrows into the idea of human sin and fallibility that informs all his work. Like a fox, he darts hither and yon to test our foibles by examining the turns and twists of history. Both dimensions are in play if we take time to look at how he viewed America. In his thought the incongruities of personal existence carry into our collective life, including that of our nation. As an American of German ancestry, Niebuhr fits well into the American story, including his rise from relative obscurity to national prominence. This chapter takes its focus from *The Irony of American History* (1952), the center of current Niebuhr interest. Teachings given voice in *The Irony of American History* draw from the depths of Niebuhr's concerns and extend through the end of his publishing career. Taking a close look at this book confirms and rounds out his message to America in the early twenty-first century.

A Classic in Context

Just as Niebuhr looked back on William James's *Varieties of Religious Experience* (1902) as a classic, we now accord similar status to some of his own books. Less well understood is the fact that classic texts in literature, philosophy, or religion have a peculiar ambivalence. Viewing them in light of a received reception easily obscures the power and vitality of their origination. Classic texts have a claim to permanence, yet their complex arguments produce divergent accounts of their meaning. In the words of philosopher Eva T. H. Brann, who has long wrestled with such works:

> Good texts rarely prejudge the first questions concerning the division of knowledge, but come before the students simply as reputable writings. And because they do not take their subject matter as given, because they so often begin by distinguishing their realm of inquiry and justifying that distinction, they further original inquiry.[1]

The Irony of American History is no exception. We're unsure of its genre, whether it belongs to history, theology, ethics, or to a form of prophetic preaching. Even if "all of the above" is correct, we remain no closer to the work's meaning. Such books, Brann argues, deserve to be read without preconditions. Vagaries in the origination and reception of such texts are easily obscured, especially when a work like *The Irony of American History* is believed to have a single dominant or even a true meaning. Reading this book is a test case for thinking about Niebuhr's present-day relevance.

Today the book is widely taken as anti-imperialist, a prescient warning against the kind of religiously-inspired, naïve idealism that led the United States into the Iraq War in 2003. That view isn't at all wrong, even if it doesn't convey a full picture of the book's meaning or its author's views on America. Written when Niebuhr was sixty, just prior to suffering a stroke that took its toll on his later years, *Irony of American History* brings into play much that he had previously written. It applies these ideas to an America that came of age during the struggle and triumph of World War II only to end up in the Cold War between the West and Stalinist Russia, each side of which had the power to destroy the earth.

Since its publication in 1952 and continuing amid the current revival of interest, *The Irony of American History* has been understood in diverse, sometimes contradictory, ways. Two initial reviewers, trained in American history, saw *Irony* as an attack on the positive achievements of liberal political traditions in the name of alien (and mistaken) ideas traceable to Karl Marx and John Calvin. Writing in the *American Quarterly,* historian Cushing Strout described the book as "a nimble manipulation of Marxism and 'bourgeois ideology' in the artificially bright glare of neo-orthodox Calvinism," while C. Page Smith, writing in the *William and Mary Quarterly,* "wonders if Mr. Niebuhr has not perhaps theologized the dialectical materialism of the nineteenth century."[2] His critics appear not to be aware of Niebuhr's commitment to the indeterminacy of history. Neither writer sees that the thrust of the book is against ideology in any of its guises. They also do not dwell long on the ironic way that Niebuhr in part honors, even as he debunks, the residual hopes of the American dream.

A prism through which the range of his teaching shines, *Irony of American History* arose at the apogee of Niebuhr's career. It brings his lifework to bear on the moral ambiguity of a nation. At one level, current readings of the book are unimpeachable. *Irony* was rediscovered amid the adventurism of an Iraq war in which America presented itself as doing good, but did so with an ideologically charged imperial design. Entire passages from the book—warnings about holy political crusades, the illusion of undertaking a preventive war, exaggerated claims of American virtue—eerily anticipate the events undertaken under George W. Bush in reaction to the September 11, 2001, attacks. Little goes unnoticed, including the ways that hysteria and psychological rationalizations feed and sustain mortal combat.

> Every nation is caught in the moral paradox of refusing to go to war unless it can be proved that the national interest is imperiled, and of continuing in the war only by proving that something much more than national interest is at stake.[3]

The single sentence captures the shift from fearing weapons of mass destruction (the famous WMD) to spreading "God-given freedom" in the world as reasons for the 2003 Bush-Cheney invasion of Iraq. It's not hard to see why current readers apply Niebuhr's acute analysis to the circumstances that surrounded the Iraq war.

> A nation with an inordinate degree of political power is doubly tempted to exceed the bounds of historical possibilities, if it is informed by an idealism which does not understand the limits of man's wisdom and volition in history.[4]
>
> Imperialism is a perennial problem of human existence; for powerful nations and individuals inevitably tend to use the weak as instruments of their purposes.[5]

Written fifty years earlier than the 2003 Iraq war, *The Irony of American History* explains our unwitting imperialism as the flip side (hence the irony) of the sense of inherent goodness in our mission to spread democracy and the cause of freedom in the world. The book regained currency when it was mentioned in David Brooks's 2007 *New York Times* column in which presidential candidate Obama cites Niebuhr as "one of his favorite philosophers" and gives a cogent summary of the theologian to the effect that trying to eliminate the evil, pain, and hardship in the world requires us to be humble and modest, though not cynical in our pursuits.[6] At the time, *Irony* was out of print. It sprang back in spring 2008 with a new introduction by diplomatic historian Andrew J. Bacevich, who maintains that "it is the most important book ever written on U.S. foreign policy."[7] That's not entirely hyperbole, even if it requires qualification. The fact is that Niebuhr's book isn't directly about foreign policy at all. It's about the ideals, myths, and illusions that cling to and distort America's self-understanding. Less obvious at the moment is the fact that *Irony* gives testimony to Niebuhr's belief in the resiliency of America's democratic practices, which can (and, he thinks, do) mute the worst excesses of the creed he criticizes.

There is reason to think that U.S. president Barack Obama not only reads Niebuhr but also takes him to heart. An approach that resists demonizing opponents and mingles tough, self-interested principles with touches of pragmatism echoes Niebuhr's political stance. Like Obama, Niebuhr is less impressed by ideology and labels than with trying to understand the actual forces at work in the world, while deciding what proximate steps might lead to a more just social order. It would undermine the intent of this book to think that Niebuhr is more relevant to the decisions of the president of the United States than to the citizenry and population generally. Not just our political leaders but an entire nation, especially one plunged into the greatest economic collapse since the 1920s, needs the hopeful realism of the theologian.

If there's a lesson for Barack Obama from Niebuhr, it lies in the view that new beginnings in history "are never quite as new as assumed, and never remain quite as pure as when they are new."[8] The American president is aware of the perils, as well as the power, of using historical analogies. His oratory has a special ability to ring the changes of history—the ideals of the founders, the reality of slavery, the anguish of Lincoln, and the vision of King—with a deftness that awakens a sense of history in others. We yearn for new beginnings and better times; sometimes they actually happen, even though we make better decisions when, in humility, we keep in mind that history unfolds with its own rhythms and surprises.

The Trajectory of a Book

Elaborating Niebuhr's themes in *Irony of American History* is like studying a Bach fugue. His points are stated with vigor, then qualified, embellished further, occasionally inverted, and finally placed in a still larger context of meaning. America is the canvas upon which Niebuhr paints, using the techniques and perspectives of his earlier work. The power of his written prose, noted earlier, is especially apparent. The book's argument fluctuates between normative claims that arise from the human condition and descriptive-historical claims about the unfolding of America's actual history. Admittedly, it's often difficult to distinguish a normative from a historical-descriptive claim, since they are so often interwoven in Niebuhr's exposition.

The Irony of American History consists of six chapters, framed by two prolonged meditations on America as ironic. Those first and last chapters are crucial to an understanding of the book's intent. In a preface Niebuhr sets off irony from pathos and tragedy by looking at the emotional dynamic of each. If I read him rightly, his intent is more to highlight the peculiar features of irony than to say that irony lacks any elements of the tragic or pathetic. Irony, as I understand Niebuhr, operates on a different plane, with greater conscious awareness on the part of the observer. Most often we respond with pity when suffering arises from natural or unavoidable causes. As noted in the previous chapter, tragedy arises in situations where evil is undertaken for the sake of good; it thus elicits admiration for its nobility and pity for its guilt. We might say that a tragic choice is ironic, once we grasp all the elements that went into its making. Ironic ways of viewing require us to discover and bring to light connections that are hidden and concealed. It's these hidden connections in irony that fascinate Niebuhr. By contrast, external incongruity is merely comic, as in the example of a pompous professor whose lecture is interrupted by a fly lighting on the tip of his nose.

Irony thus focuses on disparate aspects of our choices where individuals or nations bear responsibility for their deeds, even if an evil outcome was unintended. Irony differs from tragedy because responsibility arises more from unconscious weakness than from a conscious choice. If we are able to see the point of irony—how America as a good nation can come to do evil—the incongruity is dissolved. Irony leaves matters in ambiguity. Recognizing our complicity in unwitting evil can leave us embittered; it can also empower us with fresh impetus to deal with matters at hand. Irony only works through the mind of a critical-minded observer who can see elements of virtue as they mask vice. Although we read *The Irony of American History* as prophetic criticism of America, the stance of the prophet is one of critical observation, not moral condemnation pure and simple.

In Niebuhr's narrative (chapters 2–4) America originates amid the innocence of new beginnings, a refuge from the tyranny of Europe. The relative happiness and favorable fortune that ensue are viewed within early America as signs of divine favor and providence, though they are also the result of chance and the circumstance of being a vast continent with immense natural resources. As a result of westward expansion and manifest destiny, the sense of being originally chosen by God is enhanced and perpetuated. By the end of the nineteenth century, the Spanish American war seals this attitude of American glory with our hegemony over the Philippines and Cuba. Niebuhr views this sense of power and indomitability as "the American creed." In the twentieth century we struggle forward through the initial setbacks and eventual recovery from two world wars and the depression; we come to maturity as a nation that has lost its innocence and has assumed responsibilities commensurate with its power.

Thus far the elements of American vitality and American overreaching are both in play. The original sense of virtue as a democratic people in the new world is seen over time to have claimed too much for itself, thus ironically turning moral strength into weakness. In arguing that "experience triumphs over dogma" in chapter 5 Niebuhr is not making a general claim about American ingenuity or about American pragmatism. His claim is rather that in our practical domestic experience we have behaved better than our creed.

> Our success in establishing justice and insuring domestic tranquillity has exceeded the characteristic insights of a bourgeois culture. . . . America has developed a pragmatic approach to political and economic questions which would do credit to Edmund Burke, the great exponent of the wisdom of historical experience as opposed to the abstract rationalism of the French Revolution.[9]

The chapter marks a mental turning point in the overall argument, because it positions Niebuhr to embrace the practical aspects of American life, its robust democracy that can and does serve to correct American excesses, while still remaining critical of our overarching and overreaching posture in world affairs.

Analysis of the contest between rival ideologies, the democratic capitalism of the United States and the Marxist-Leninist ideology of the Soviet Union, is then presented in chapter 6. The appeal of communism to the earth's poor and impoverished people is likened to a religious utopia that consigns its subjects to a cruel and all-powerful state. There follows a set of potential warnings and musings about "the American future" in chapter 7. Against the background of a morally ambiguous America, a searching eight-page section focuses on the danger of launching a preventive strike against Russia and champions the restraint of Niebuhr's friend and political associate George F. Kennan in shaping U.S. policy.[10] Having come of age to witness the rise of Hitler's terror, followed by Stalinist ideology and nuclear stalemate with the USSR, Niebuhr worked to foster the containment policy of Kennan within state-department circles. Indeed, hatred of communism was as pervasive and strong then as today's hatred, fear, and confusion regarding the peril of radical political Islamism. At the time Niebuhr's stance required more sobriety and courage than we are able to realize in retrospect.

Finally, Niebuhr writes chapter 8 on the relationship of irony to history, to the Christian faith, and to political-historical thinking generally. The final chapter repays careful study. It asks whether irony can only be used for such analysis by appealing as a Christian to a universal framework of meaning, that is, the divine perspective on all human history, or whether irony presents a viable way of looking at America in a nonreligious perspective. Niebuhr thus anticipates a central concern within his work, even as he leaves the answer to his question to be determined by his readers.

Virtue and Prosperity

In the 1950s with a newly elected war hero, President Eisenhower, America exuded the promise and confidence of its original destiny. John Winthrop's famous sermon "A City on a Hill" espouses a special sense of destiny for America, reinforced by the idea that in this country—unlike others—anything is possible. The "city on a hill" rhetoric continues its merry way on the political circuit or virtually anywhere that it usefully attests to one's sense of American patriotism.

So how did all this look in the era of Niebuhr?

It's no accident that Niebuhr wrote the words "nothing worth doing can be achieved in our lifetime; therefore we must be saved by hope" in a chapter on "Happiness, Prosperity, and Virtue." He felt deeply that Americans "may be too secure in both our sense of power and our sense of virtue to be ready to engage in a patient chess game with the recalcitrant forces of historic destiny."[11] In this regard, Americans are emblematic of the modern West, which

> lacks the humility to accept the fact that the whole drama of history is enacted in a frame of meaning too large for human comprehension or management. It is a drama in which fragmentary meanings can be discerned within a penumbra of mystery. . . . [12]

Niebuhr's thought reminds his readers that ancient civilizations, like China and India, know the lesson of patience better than do Americans. He maintains that Europeans know the lesson better than Americans, and that our kinsmen, the British, generally do so as well. All seem more able to chart a course for the distant future, less swayed by immediate political consequences.

These themes occur repeatedly in *Irony,* but come to a head in chapter 4. Whether Calvinist or Jeffersonian, "belief in the perfect compatibility of virtue and prosperity" seems implicit in the American character. Like Tocqueville in the 1830s, Niebuhr sees the links between American worldliness and our moral and religious values. Our religiosity and idealism have long been curiously linked with materialism in ways that baffle outside observers. Jeffersonians held that prosperity and well-being should be sought as the basis of virtue, while the Puritans regarded virtue as the basis of prosperity.

> But in any case the fusion of these two forces created a preoccupation with the material circumstances of life which expressed a more consistent bourgeois ethos than that of even the most advanced nations of Europe.[13]

A page later, Niebuhr elaborates as follows:

> Our difficulty as a nation is that we must now learn that prosperity is not simply coordinated to virtue, and that virtue is not simply coordinated to historic destiny and that happiness is no simple possibility of human existence.[14]

It is tempting to dwell at length on the age-old presumption that material well-being and personal virtue go together. In writing about "Happiness, Prosperity, and Virtue" Niebuhr is aware that the tendency to associate material well-being with righteous behavior refuses to go away.

The expectation of immediate rewards for good behavior runs deep; it seems virtually to belong to our natural consciousness as humans. The Bible gives it expression, even as it strongly protests against it. The would-be friends of Job chastise him for refusing to see the correlation between being upright and being well-off.

> Think now, who that was innocent has ever perished?
> Or where were the upright cut off?
> As I have seen, those who plow iniquity and sow trouble
> reap the same. (Eliphaz, in Job 4:7–8)

For Niebuhr, as for Job, the ways of history and of deity are mysterious. Life cannot be sustained over the long haul if it rests on the expectation of steady and harmonious existence. In chapter 2 we saw that Nassim Nicholas Taleb in *Fooled by Randomness* and Malcom Gladwell in *Outliers* question the widespread assumption of a simple correlation between our deeds and good fortune and view it as a cultural fiction.

Niebuhr's point is not that all of life is random. That would make it impossible to have basic trust with loved ones, let alone have decent transnational relationships in the larger human community. Along with Taleb, he holds that more seems random than we may want to acknowledge. There is something to be said for keeping some relationship between moral character and economic well-being. Good habits, especially those of modest and careful decision-making, carry over from individuals to societal institutions. Niebuhr knew that basic trust and inner honesty lie at the heart of human well-being. It's just that these qualities so readily go awry in human affairs. Knowing more about that process, he thinks, better prepares us to structure our lives and communities in ways that may be less damaging to our fellow human beings.

Wrapping up his discussion of prosperity and virtue, Niebuhr reminds us that "happiness is desired by all men; and moments of it are probably attained by most men. Only moments of it can be attained because happiness is the inner concomitant of neat harmonies of body, spirit and society; and these neat harmonies are bound to be infrequent."[15]

Power, Economics, and Politics

Americans don't do well in coming to grips with power. The ideology of equality overlooks the fact that economic power is a major factor in

America. Books with titles like "Who Rules America?" are used as college texts but don't have much impact in shaping society. Talking as if social class plays a role in the lives of individuals, even acknowledging social class in America, seems heretical and off-putting in American political rhetoric. Niebuhr put the matter succinctly in writing that "privileged classes tried to preserve the illusion of classical liberalism that power is not an important element in man's social life."[16] He is aware that the idea of the kingdom of God has powerful earthly repercussions, even if the ideal kingdom never fully comes to pass. Certainly, on religious grounds, the kingdom is not brought about by humans acting politically, however noble and just their ideals. Niebuhr holds that "our own culture is schizophrenic on the subject of power."[17] His point that "economic power is more covert than political or military power" is telling.[18] Power and dominance are less obvious in the financial world than in sectors of public life. Since financial and business interests offer jobs and products that are useful, while reinforcing the virtue of their operations through limitless advertising, we are inclined to think of them as "socially neutral" or benign. Yet that is far from the case for Niebuhr. Characteristically, he writes:

> Every ethical and social problem of a just distribution of the privileges of life is solved by so enlarging the privileges that either an equitable distribution is made easier, or a lack of equity is rendered less noticeable.[19]

Niebuhr anticipated the rhetoric of "trickle down economics" that would allow privilege to grow through tax breaks, while concealing the effects of those policies on those less fortunate. He thus challenged the popular view (in the 1950s and since) that a rational harmony of interests is America's natural condition. We've seen the significance of the "equality of sin, inequality of guilt" theme in Niebuhr's theology. On that view not all sin and social evil is equally culpable and damaging to the human community. Those with more responsibility, whose decisions affect large numbers of people, err more grandly. They also incur more guilt, provided that they have enough inner honesty in regard to their deeds. Even where the weight of guilt goes unacknowledged, which seems to be the case in the 2008–2009 financial debacle, the deeds of subterfuge, scam, and swindle have devastated the lives of individuals and groups of investors.

The dream of a just society looms large in American ideology. We touch on it next under the heading of Exceptionalism. We may hope or dream about a situation of simple justice with quid pro quo social and economic equality. A one-time socialist, Niebuhr saw the impossibility of such justice to be directed by the state, even as he criticizes the illusions that the economic exchanges of the market are ever just by themselves. In *The Irony of American History* he holds that "there is no neat principle which will solve the relation of power to justice and of justice to freedom."[20] He rejects the harsh slogans and illusions of Marx (very much alive in the Communist world of 1952) and of Adam Smith's invisible hand (currently taking a beating in the United States). Political experience must prudently seek to create approximations of justice in light of the ideal of love and needs of the human community.

Chapter 6 on "The International Class Struggle" is the most dated part of Niebuhr's book, though the absence of living Marxist dogma in today's world makes his analysis stand out all the more poignantly. Niebuhr argues that the relative success of the American labor movement since the New Deal has refuted the Marxian dogma regarding the exploitation of the working class at the hands of the business class. Read today, however, chapter 6 has a different message. It reminds us that the rights and protections of working-class America for a decent living, hard-won contracts of labor unions, and guarantees for health care have been curtailed, if not all but vanished, since Niebuhr's day.

Niebuhr warns against looking for single causal agents or isolated villains in history. At the same time, he knows it is the nature of nations to be self-righteous and to justify their actions, based on legitimate self-interest. It's hard to grasp the messiness of political reality.

> We can understand the neat logic of either economic reciprocity or the show of pure power. But we are mystified by the endless complexities of human motives and the varied compounds of ethnic loyalties, cultural traditions, social hopes, envies and fears which enter into the policies of nations, and which lie at the foundation of their political cohesion.[21]

The passage shows us the complexity of Niebuhr's analysis. He deals in theory (political philosophies, large historical interpretations, his own view of human sin and fallibility) while attending to multifarious factors. His practical temperament and activism urge political forces to get things done that are possible to do. It's a mistake to see his criticism of intellectualism as anti-intellectual. Theory and analysis have a great deal to do with shaping U.S. history. But better intellects, without honesty, trust, and a sense of limits, will not get us far. Niebuhr absorbed the lesson of St. Augustine that pride works in our mental lives as much as through our bodies. Human intellectuality offers a mighty way to extend the ego and is no more free from pride and pretension than any other human endeavor.

We've observed that Niebuhr defends American democracy in relative terms and believes that our practices are often superior to our creed. He offers two caveats to his view that our experience as Americans generally triumphs over dogma.[22] In the first Niebuhr expresses concern that the pristine status of property rights in the United States, then under attack by Soviet ideology, conceals ways in which property is in fact used unjustly in power relationships. If the Marxist ideology is more monstrous, thinks Niebuhr, this arises because it recognizes no distinctions between economic and political power.

In his second caveat Niebuhr bluntly warns about the dangers of the creed of free market capitalism.

> The lip service which the whole culture pays to the principles of *laissez-faire* makes for tardiness in dealing with the instability of a free economy, when the perils of inflation or deflation arise. They are finally dealt with pragmatically; but not before the consequences of inaction have become very apparent.

He continues by writing presciently: "Some believe that the lessons taught in the great depression of 1929 have been so well learned that a recurrence of such a catastrophe is impossible; but it is not altogether certain that this is true," and as a result of our potential economic instability "we remain an irritatingly incalculable element in world stability."[23] The practice of turning legitimate theoretical debate into narrow doctrinal positions changes thought into ideology in ways that endanger the foundations of a democratic society.

Theoretical postures assume seductive rhetorical forms ("defense of privacy," "individual rights," "the free market," and "the American Dream"). For Niebuhr, the "business class" goes about its work blithely oblivious to the corrosive effects of the free market ideology that guides its pursuits. It is ironic that we believe we are a nation of individuals, when in fact so many Americans endorse the same large sets of ideas and myths about themselves as a people. Officially we say we are a practical people, who stand against of all kinds of "-isms." Communism and fascism, the largest "-isms" of Niebuhr's day, are passé as virulent ideologies. But American nationalism—under the guise of patriotism—is so widely taken for granted that it seems to reign supreme. Rediscovery of *The Irony of American History* began as the "war on terror" was running its course. Wars against abstractions are inevitably based on ideology, hence on abstract fear and illusions, more than on reality. The "evils against which we contend are frequently the fruit of illusions which are similar to our own."[24]

Niebuhr repeatedly takes up America's apparent faith that social science can provide solutions to our deepest quandaries. As we've seen, the discriminating center of humans, which freely weighs moral options, cannot be grasped by quantitative methods, even when pursued at their best. That is not the pious wish of a theologian, but a reasoned claim about the decision-making of humans as free moral agents. Even with expert polling techniques we are incapable of predicting human behavior. Large intellectual constructs—ideologies—run roughshod over human experience. In Niebuhr's day those constructs were Karl Marx versus Adam Smith. The former is no longer upheld as viable, and the latter symbol of the free market has now come to be questioned in ways unforeseen since the 1930s, or indeed, the 1950s.

Patriotism and Exceptionalism

If a modicum of balance in power relations is crucial for America's economic and political health, the same holds for a sense of national pride in country. In connection with the new Obama era in American politics, we've noted elements of idealism that may—or may not—fit easily into the patterns of Niebuhr's thought. At times U.S. political campaigns seem obsessed with upholding patriotism and the American Dream as rhetorical litmus tests for candidates. As debunker and realist, Niebuhr seems to move in another direction entirely. It behooves us to look at what he says about both patriotism (love of country) and exceptionalism (uniqueness of America) as a way of further taking his bearings on America.

Although it doesn't come up directly in *The Irony of American History,* the topic of patriotism came up early in Niebuhr's thought as he wrestled with the morality of individuals and groups, including nations. In *Moral Man and Immoral Society* he poses what he calls "the ethical paradox" of patriotism through which "patriotism transmutes individual unselfishness into national egoism." The argument goes like this:

> Loyalty to the nation is a high form of altruism when compared with lesser loyalties and more parochial interests. It therefore becomes the vehicle of all the altruistic impulses and expresses itself, on occasion, with such fervor that the critical attitude of the individual toward the nation

> and its enterprises is almost completely destroyed. The unqualified character of this devotion is the very basis of the nation's power and of the freedom to use the power without moral restraint. Thus the unselfishness of individuals makes for the selfishness of nations.[25]

Niebuhr's analysis of how individual unselfishness is sublimated into a "my country right or wrong" attitude traces the moves within the human self as it seeks to justify belief in nation as the highest entity. Idolatry, putting something limited or "finite" in place of deity, is the most pervasive sort of sin. On the overall point in question, his appeal to a still larger horizon of meaning, a God or universal moral law, is the only remedy at hand to ward off extreme nationalisms. That is in fact what Niebuhr argues as a whole about American and other forms of nationalism. He rejected his earlier pacifism when he saw what Hitler was up to. His championing of our entry into the battle against Hitler indicated a belief not just that America was worthy of being defended, but that the morality of the world order was itself under attack.

In turning to Niebuhr on American exceptionalism we take up the idea of the American Dream, seeing the United States as a unique nation with a special role and destiny in world history. The idea remains alive in the twenty-first century. Its message often takes the form of touting our freedom from tyranny, the founding motif of the American revolution. The U.S. Constitution, the oldest charter of a thriving democratic system of government, enshrines these values. It is widely thought in popular American culture that liberties are more apt to be protected here than in other nations. Grassroots political rhetoric suggests that we are the "greatest country on earth," apparently without any sense of comparative insight into health care or the income gap between rich and poor. "America was a harbinger of the perfect world which was in the making," writes Niebuhr, while reminding us that, "there is a deep layer of messianic consciousness in the mind of America."[26] Our founding documents exude an idealism of new beginnings, a promise that "the pursuit of happiness" is an "inalienable right."

Indeed, distinguished scholars hold that we are a "natural rights republic," based upon a unique distillation of political teaching that inspires hope for other societies and nation-states.[27] On this view the classical eighteenth-century Enlightenment left a mark upon the founding culture and ideals of the United States that still makes America the envy of much of the world. Historian Louis P. Masur notes that accounts are starting to challenge the idea of American exceptionalism by seeking to integrate the story of the

United States into transnational narratives that include other nations. We are, after all, not the only nation of immigrants, as any student of Brazil, to cite an example, must know. Other historians, sociologists, political scientists, including Simon Schama in *The American Future: A History* (2009), continue to write about "the American Dream" and the example of Barack Obama as demonstrating that the idea has currency and appeal, not just domestically but around the world.[28] The campaign of Barack Obama reinforced the sense of America as exceptional in the rhetoric that states that "only here . . . only now, in this place" could someone of mixed ethnicity with a Kenyan father and a Kansas mother rise to the presidency. Around the 2008 November election, European pundits and writers tacitly acknowledged that, for all their liberalism, no person of mixed race would have a similar chance in the political systems of Britain, France, or Germany.

Apart from the odyssey of its new president, American exceptionalism has generally been in retreat.[29] But history has given it a reprieve and new prominence with the collapse of communism and the emergence of new geopolitical realities since the 1990s. It was given a bad name under the presidency of George W. Bush as the United States turned away from negotiated settlements and traditional ties to Europe, while insisting that we go it alone. As a result, historian of international affairs and Niebuhr admirer Andrew J. Bacevich insists that the sense of American uniqueness feeds the kind of crusading spirit and messianism that lay behind our response to the attacks of 9/11. He makes the argument at length in *The Limits of Power: The End of American Exceptionalism* (2008). Bacevich is hardly alone. Other recent titles make comparable arguments: Fareed Zakaria, *The Post-America World* (2008) and Parak Khanna, *The Second World: How Emerging Powers Are Redefining Global Competition in the Twenty-first Century* (2009). Written with the scope (and detailed knowledge) of Arnold Toynbee, Khanna's geopolitical realism argues that, as a matter of survival, the traces of American exceptionalism must be transformed, if not buried. In the global economic community that unfolds, post-Obama, the European Community and China will play a role at least equal to, if not ahead of, the United States on the world stage. Zakaria and Khanna both insist that a more modest America will, in the end, be a stronger America. Leading the way toward more global interpretations of America is the work of Daniel T. Rodgers, *Atlantic Crossings: Social Politics in a Progressive Age* (Harvard, 1998), which calls for the history of the United States to be written "within a world of transnational historical forces."[30]

In the end, the suspicion is that for Niebuhr, as for many Americans, the debate about being patriotic or thinking America is unique tries to capture complexities that don't yield simple results. The late sociologist Seymour Martin Lipset, in *American Exceptionalism* (1995), offered wise counsel in pointing out that "exceptionalism is a two-edged phenomenon: it does not mean better."[31] Lipset continued by pointing out the sheer differentness at work in the United States as an "outlier," with belief in human rights, religion, individualism, and the highest participation in voluntary organizations, but also with the highest crime rates and number of incarcerations in the world, plus the lowest voter turnout among democracies. Lipset's analysis of the discrepancies between the American ideal and social-political-economic reality goes beyond Niebuhr in sociological detail. Yet the sense of incongruity that had led the theologian to his ironic perspective remains in Lipset's discussion.

The debate about American exceptionalism cuts through the center of America's ability to grasp what it is as a nation. It's as if one side has a primal faith, anchored in patriotism and military service, that the country and its values are exemplary in all fundamental respects. The other side, often consisting of people who have spent more time living overseas, knows that there is much in the United States that falls far short of its own ideals. For such persons, it is not necessary to deride or derail the American dream in order to point out the discrepancies.

In fact, something like that approach was taken by Niebuhr in the 1950s. He was critical of America, called for a realism that was represented by John Adams and James Madison, yet knew that the founding ideals of the nation are also what gave resilience to our national life during the Civil War and work of Lincoln. It's important to get the two aspects of Niebuhr's argument right, because to err on this point is to miss him entirely, or to claim him wrongly for something he never espoused. Niebuhr was himself the model of a harsh critic and strong defender of America. The same was true of his contemporary George F. Kennan, and the immigrant political philosopher, Hans J. Morgenthau.

The Standpoint of Irony

It may seem strange that a Protestant Christian theologian is fond of using the term "irony" in connection with history and politics. Typically we associate irony with literature. As a rhetorical trope it has the effect of conveying something other than a literal meaning. Irony also has broad ramifications. It was put to good use by Kierkegaard, who felt a similar need to talk about incongruities and discrepancies between the human heart and the world of society. By invoking irony Niebuhr appeals to a sensibility of individuals that can be applied both to individuals and to groups. "There is no simple congruity between the ideals of sensitive individuals and the moral mediocrity of even the best society."[32] Only individuals can appreciate irony, which functions mainly as a tool of retrospective insight. Something is said or done, and we say—after the fact—that it was ironic. A U.S. foreign policy stance may arise from an ironic situation and have ironic results, but it isn't planned that way. When Niebuhr tells us that "we could not be virtuous . . . if we were really as innocent as we pretend to be," he reminds us that virtue loses some of its purity when put into practice in the world.[33] Irony enables Niebuhr to acknowledge human complexity and the mixture of good and evil in the moral life.

If the awareness of discrepancies and contradictory levels of meaning become visible only after the fact, seeing the world through irony also has lessons for the future. If we become aware of a tendency to conceal what we would prefer not to reveal (about ourselves or our country), this insight may well guide future actions. As Niebuhr sees America, irony arises when yearning to do good, pursued in extremes, becomes rigid and rides roughshod over the sensibilities of others. Pride in feeling oneself doing good readily slips into hubris and a sense of superiority over those not involved in our cause. Virtue turns into vice when we become overly confident. An ironic sense of self includes a sense of guilt and moral responsibility. It stands between pure pathos and pure tragedy. As we've seen, pathos arises when we helplessly confront necessity, tragedy when a heroic actor sacrifices self for a greater good. As a tool of insight, irony thus holds together contradictions. That's why it's especially useful for a realist perspective that refuses to choose between optimism and pessimism.

The spate of recent books on American militarism and American empire that cite Niebuhr do not dwell on his sense of irony.[34] Most of these writers (Andrew J. Bacevich, Gary Dorrien, Michael Ignatieff, Chalmers Johnson, Clyde V. Prestowitz and Cornel West) decry our imperial ambitions, as if they can somehow be limited, if not abandoned, though some (Niall Ferguson) call for a new American maturity that would have the courage of nineteenth-century Britain to pursue empire with confidence. Irony allows Niebuhr to get beyond pure outrage and moral condemnation. An ironic perspective enables him to offer devastating criticism, while recognizing that our moral perils do not arise from "conscious malice or the explicit lust for power. They are the perils which can be understood only if we realize the ironic tendency of virtues to turn into vices when too complacently relied upon."[35] Like individuals, nations are even more caught up in hypocrisy and self-righteousness. Seeing answers to these problems only occurs—if it occurs at all—to the individual human self, as the significant unit of thought and action in history.[36] In the end, Niebuhr believes that only the perspective of faith in a reality higher than self and nation can dissipate the incongruities of history.[37] If the classical Protestant answer to the ambiguity of human sin is a call for repentance and new beginnings, the paradigm continues to work—even if less overtly—in Niebuhr's ironic political analyses.

If we try to sum up a revisit to America through the eyes of Niebuhr, his notion of history repeating itself, though never in exactly the same way, seems to stand up. Nowhere is Niebuhr's ability to turn a phrase better exhibited than in *The Irony of American History.* Of course, a word about why Niebuhr sees American history as ironic is in order. His repeated examples from the fears and anxieties of the Cold War show us how America's confidence, idealism, and power can so easily and unwittingly turn into vice, even wreak havoc in damaging ways. Irony preserves the tensions of Niebuhr's perspective on human life as both wonderful and fallible. How this relates to his larger religious and Christian orientation is taken up in the next two chapters. Here, it's important to see that irony, for all its critical posture, is something more than negative judgment. It's a tool that gives us insight into our nation as well as our own individual lives as these embody the tensions and conflicts between the ideal and the real.

Near the end of his career Niebuhr continued to take stock of overreaching pride in the life of nations. His last major book, *The Structure of Nations and Empires* (1959), carried the argument about imperialism and ideology into a comparative study of the United States and the USSR. Neither nation, so Niebuhr argues, could admit to its imperial ambitions. The United States could not do so, because its notion of democracy forbids it, and the Soviets could not do so because Marxism held that the category only applies to the capitalist world. The implied parallelism between the two nations should give pause to writers on the right who downplay Niebuhr's criticism of America while seeing him as hawkish on the Communists.

It's no secret why Niebuhr is again being read by political theorists and persons charged with shaping the future of America. Many of these figures, including Brent Scowcroft and Joseph Nye, repeatedly weighed in on the

Iraq war. A return to Niebuhr, as theologian and ethicist, is happening because of what he has to say, but also how he says it. The final sentences of *The Irony of American History* state in ominous terms the fate of a great nation that ignores the real struggles that it faces.

> For if we should perish, the ruthlessness of the foe would be only the secondary cause of the disaster. The primary cause would be that the strength of a giant nation was directed by eyes too blind to see all the hazards of the struggle; and the blindness would be induced not by some accident of nature or history, but by hatred and vainglory.[38]

In *Ethical Realism: A Vision for America's Role in the World* (2006), liberal and conservative political analysts Anatol Lieven and John Hulsman join forces to invoke Niebuhr alongside the realists among political philosophers, Hans J. Morgenthau and George F. Kennan. But it is Niebuhr, in the words just cited, to whom they turn for the epigraph of their final chapter. Those words gain their power from the same faith tradition and transcendent moral vision that animated Lincoln and Martin Luther King.

On the task of appealing to Niebuhr on behalf of a current ideology or an explicit policy stance, a word of caution is warranted. As he once put it: "Reliance upon historical analogy is frequently unreflective."[39] Having a full and rounded view of Niebuhr's America equips readers to judge for themselves among the uses of his name by current writers and pundits. In the end, we can argue that Niebuhr on America has mainly, though not entirely, been vindicated. A preventive war against the Soviet Union, against which he warned, did not materialize. That prescient warning along with his strictures on the arrogance of power subsequently found their mark in the presidency of George W. Bush. At the same time, Niebuhr's confidence in the relatively just dealings of America's business class with working people and trade unions has not held up in the intervening decades. From this we see that his pronouncements, like all others, cannot be taken as if frozen in time. History, as he teaches us to believe, is forever inconclusive. It continues to work its will in surprising ways, as the 2008 election of Barack Obama has shown.

6

DEBATING POLITICS AND THE CHRISTIAN FAITH

We all may derive rewarding insights from the Christian conception of man without accepting the Christian drama of sin and salvation as true, but to a believer this is probably a fairly idiotic position. . . . An irreligious age is left in a helpless position; but at least Dr. Niebuhr can give a coherent explanation of how it got that way.

Arthur M. Schlesinger, Jr., reviewing *Discerning the Signs of the Times* in the *Nation* (June 22, 1946)

It is at this point [thinking about the moral life] that I part company with many theologians who tend to deal with the Christian life as though it were somehow discontinuous with other modes of human existence.

H. Richard Niebuhr, Yale theologian and brother of Reinhold, in *The Responsible Self: An Essay in Christian Moral Philosophy* (1963)

We've seen the relevance of irony to Niebuhr's thinking about America's moral ambiguity. The long-term promise of John Winthrop's City on a Hill to the wider world—or to its own citizens—remains unfinished business. To invoke a favorite Niebuhr verse from St. Paul, we view the course of human affairs "through a glass darkly." If human ambiguity is a dominant Niebuhrian motif, versions of the theme are echoed in the contentious reception given his legacy by U.S. Protestant theologians and shapers of Christian opinion. Arthur Schlesinger, Jr., spoke for many agnostics in puzzling over how Niebuhr's wisdom on human nature relates to his Christian theology. The issue of whether and how Niebuhr's worldly wisdom relates to his understanding of the traditional claims of Christian faith has perplexed humanists and Christians alike, beginning in his lifetime. Today's reception of Niebuhr among Christians presents a mixed picture. Just at a time when political pundits believe he is the man of the hour as critic of American imperialism and a beam of political realism for

Barack Obama, Niebuhr's reception within U.S. Protestantism ranges from approval and indifference to outspoken, combative hostility. A wide gulf exists between Niebuhr's current political admirers and his theological detractors. Radically different assumptions hold sway not only over secular approaches to politics, but within the craft of shaping Christian theological thinking. This is especially the case since theology, if it has any integrity, must seek its justification on grounds other than its appeal to secularists. Some of these issues have already been adumbrated. I began this book in chapter 1 by mapping the revival of interest in Niebuhr's politics; chapter 3 makes clear that his Pauline and Augustinian teaching on sin goes against the grain of modernity, even for many Christians. Now it's time to delve more directly into the intra-Christian controversies that haunt Niebuhr's teaching. The task of exploring the contours of Niebuhr reception among U.S. Christians partly, though not entirely, echoes issues that were in play during his lifetime. Taking on this task helps us round out a sense of his teaching and its ongoing status in the public arena of American Christianity.

Admittedly, Niebuhr is a tough pill to swallow. His Christian language confuses some readers and is viewed as insufficiently orthodox by others. To the extent that we grasp his teaching, he presents us with hard choices. Niebuhr calls upon us to take a serious moral inventory of ourselves, of the institutions that surround us, and of our nation. His teaching challenges an optimism that is embedded in American popular religion and in the business culture of a commercial civilization. Niebuhr challenges rival faiths—evangelical and liberal Christianity, pristine forms of Christian orthodoxy, megachurch piety—and the belief that the achievements of science and technology fundamentally alter the nature and challenges of human existence. Not surprisingly, his views have relatively more resonance among Christians who are formed by Lutheran, Calvinist, or Catholic traditions, where traces of historic Christian teachings on relating to the world tend to reside.

An Ambiguous Reception

It's uncertain whether Niebuhr's newer political admirers would register shock, confusion, or just indifference if they read widely in the extant criticism of Niebuhr. Many of these admirers are themselves deeply engaged with their own religious faith. *Washington Post* writer E. J. Dionne, Jr., a Roman Catholic schooled by the Benedictines, is surely wrong when he stated at a *Speaking of Faith* forum at Georgetown University in January 2009, that "all God's children are Niebuhrians." That was never the case in Niebuhr's lifetime, and it's hardly the case today. In her book, *The Serenity Prayer: Faith and Politics in Times of Peace and War,* Niebuhr's daughter, Elisabeth Sifton, reminds us that her father, like Paul Tillich, wasn't all that popular among the churches, despite their following among intellectuals and the reading public.

> I am regularly amazed when I read in this or that magazine that my father, like his friend Paul Tillich, was a 'major leader' of postwar American Protestantism. If only! American Protestant churches mostly paid the two of them no heed. A small minority of intrepid souls may have enjoyed having my father vent his feisty views on the need for racial equality, for a committed curriculum of social justice, for a radical reorganization of industrial democracy. . . . But most of them simply didn't want to listen. Ministers all over America might have been pounding the lecterns and delivering fire-and-brimstone sermons, but their social conformism was pretty complete.[1]

Sorting out how Niebuhr is viewed within today's Christian world is no simple task. Labels given to theological trends and movements are as difficult to unravel as their counterparts in the political arena. What follows gives a sketch of the main tendencies of endorsing, sidestepping, or seeking to supplant the legacy of Niebuhr in today's Protestant Christian world. I am not here talking about resistance to Niebuhr just because his teaching is hard—which it is. I am rather talking about Christian resistance to Niebuhr that arises because of differing assumptions about religion, the Christian faith, issues of war and peace, and the most authentic way of fulfilling the moral responsibilities of the Christian life.

It provides perspective if we recognize that the issues in question have haunted the Christian movement since the first century. Like political philosophy, Christian theology is always a work in progress, subject to historical interests and shifting objectives and concerns. In H. Richard Niebuhr's now classic, *Christ and Culture* (1951), Reinhold Niebuhr's brother offered a five-fold account of the ways that the Christian tradition has interacted with culture. More ambitious in scope than *The Irony of American History* (1952), the book maps the contours of the entire Christian tradition.[2] Its masterful fivefold ("ideal-typical") typology, inspired by Max Weber and Ernst Troeltsch, identifies the major ways that the Christian movement has attempted to relate the church to the world. In the hands of H. Richard

Niebuhr the categories of full assimilation (Christ of culture) and world rejection (Christ against culture) bookend the quasi-historical grid by pointing to Christians who have been wholly assimilated to the world ("cultural Christians") and those who reject the world ("separatists"). To H. Richard Niebuhr, Unitarian-Universalists would typically fit into the former category, while the Amish into the latter. In between such extremes, H. Richard Niebuhr thinks the majority of Christians fall into the camps of "paradoxical dualism" (Christ in paradox with culture), "synthesizing harmony" (Christ above culture), and "conversionism" (Christ transforming culture). As exponents of these latter three categories Luther is characterized as a paradoxical dualist, Thomas Aquinas, Richard Hooker and the High Church rationalists as synthesizers, and Augustine and Calvin as transformationists.

I bring up the five-fold characterization, since it reminds us that the Christian tradition has never uniformly expressed the meaning and implications of its faith in relation to the larger society. The typology was not intended to be an exact guide, but to point out the variety of ways that Christians have proposed to relate to the world around them. Ever since the book's publication, most readers have placed Reinhold Niebuhr in the "dualist" camp alongside Luther. Members of this group "seek to do justice to the need for holding together as well as for distinguishing between loyalty to Christ and responsibility for culture."[3] That works for Niebuhr, though his hope for change in the world made him critical of the passivity of Luther's social and political teaching.[4] Niebuhr does more than revel in Christian paradox. The Pauline injunction, "perplexed, but not driven to despair" (2 Cor. 4:8) states his overall posture. For him the Christian faith stands in a troubled relationship to culture, yet calls for measured steps toward social justice, even though the hope of perfection on earth remains illusory. Critics of Niebuhr who resolutely carry the message of Jesus's self-sacrificial love into the world in a transformative manner deny that they are "against the world" as sectarians. Whatever one may finally think of H. Richard Niebuhr's typology, bringing it into our discussion shows that no single sort of Christian attitude toward the world has entirely prevailed over others—a lesson worth keeping in mind today.

Like that of his brother H. Richard Niebuhr, Reinhold Niebuhr's work continues to be read, examined, and debated among Christian ethicists and theologians who teach in universities and divinity schools. Even if intellectual fashions have changed and developed within theology, the work of the Niebuhrs continues to be poured over and analyzed at professional conferences of the American Academy of Religion, in pages of the *Journal of Religious Ethics,* and at annual meetings of the Society of Christian Ethics. The fact that a "Reinhold Niebuhr Society" dedicated to the study of his legacy was first introduced in 2003 within the American Academy of Religion, the largest professional group of theologians and religion scholars, signals the renewed vitality of fresh interest. Some secular readers of this book doubtless view the whole of theology as a witches' brew, scarcely worth sampling. But in an era of global religious resurgence and turmoil, not to mention ever-present anxiety about church-state relations in the United States, a look at critics and detractors of Niebuhr's Christian thought throws further light on his teaching.

Although Niebuhr turned away from the liberal periodical the *Christian Century* in the 1940s (over the issue of "isolationism") to found his own journal *Christianity and Crisis,* the voices of Dennis McCann, James Wall, and Martin Marty have for some years discussed Niebuhrian perspectives in the *Christian Century.* Today Niebuhr is heralded and recognized most strongly by Christian intellectuals within mainstream liberal Protestantism, even though a sense of Christian unease, ranging from disinterest to hostility, surrounds Niebuhr's name on a wider stage.

Today's Protestant Christian movements generally relate to or ignore Niebuhr based upon how they see the work of the church relating to the political world and whether they find Niebuhr an adequate guide to the practice of church-based discipleship. An illuminating case of ambiguity toward Niebuhr is seen in the popular movement of *Sojourners,* based in Washington, D.C., and led by Jim Wallis, author of the best-selling books *God's Politics: Why the Right Gets It Wrong and the Left Doesn't Get It* (2005) and *The Great Awakening: Reviving Faith and Politics in a Post-Religious Right America* (2008).[5] Founder of the Sojourners movement, Wallis emerged from the Plymouth Brethren, the fundamentalist-evangelical background of Garrison Keillor. For years Wallis has labored to relate the Christian faith to seeking justice, especially for the poor and downtrodden in urban America. Thoroughly up-to-date in internet use, the Sojo movement issues daily bulletins to its subscribers in the form of scripture lessons, enjoinments to seek social justice, and comments on key stories in the daily news. Wallis, who is the leading builder of bridges between environmentalists and evangelicals, has a significant following among younger U.S. Christians. Without espousing pacifism on principle, the peace-urging Sojourners movement was against the 2003 war in Iraq and urges caution in all U.S. overseas adventures.

To an observer, Sojourners Christians are engaging the cause of pursuing justice in the world, an agenda that was endorsed repeatedly by Niebuhr against a self-satisfied, complacent Protestantism. Yet they are indifferent, if not hostile, to Niebuhr's teaching. A March 1987 *Sojourners* cover story depicted Niebuhr as an "Apologist of Power" who does not put "faithfulness before effectiveness." Instead of practicing Jesus's sacrificial love in the world ("giving witness to Christ"), Niebuhr is said to choose "the lesser of two evils." Sojourners Christians assess the mission of the church with less suspicion than Niebuhr. They want a Christian community that is more uplifting, engaged directly with issues of poverty, homelessness, and grassroots social justice, while seeking to transform lives, often despite or against the world of politics. Although they may look like "separatists," their Christ is a deeply engaged witness for justice over against the larger culture.

It's odd that the movement around Jim Wallis doesn't cite Niebuhr, though honors "witnesses to the faith" influenced by him, including Martin Luther King, Myles Horton (civil rights pioneer and founder of the Highlander research center in Tennessee), Dietrich Bonhoeffer, and Jimmy Carter.[6] In fact, Sojourners is focused more on engaging with the world than in doctrinal quarrels with other Christians. It generally represents grassroots Christian renewal, though there are signs of an increasing aspiration to speak with some impact to the halls of power. In *The Call to Conversion* Jim Wallis states:

> At heart, I am a nineteenth-century evangelical; I was just born in the wrong century. The evangelical Christians of the nineteenth century combined revivalism with social reform and helped lead campaigns to abolish slavery and support women's suffrage and child labor laws. . . . Today poverty is the new slavery—imprisoning bodies, minds, and souls—destroying hope and ending the future for a generation.[7]

That is well, good, and admirable in a Niebuhrian perspective, even if it does not fully make the connections between the corruption of individual lives and the larger corrupt structures of our political and economic existence. There is little mention of sin in Jim Wallis's books. At the outset of his career, Niebuhr broke with the Social Gospel movement of Walter Rauschenbusch who, he believed, did not have an adequate understanding of the structures of institutional sin in the world or a way of addressing such issues. At present Sojourners is more Social Gospel than Niebuhr, though the evidence isn't fully in on that score, and the religious and evangelical scene is shifting rapidly.[8] An article by Laurie Goodstein in the *New York*

Times (Sunday, March 15, 2009) reported that the Reverend Jim Wallis is one of five evangelical clergy who have been cultivated by Barack Obama "for private prayer sessions on the telephone and for discussions on the role of religion in politics." At the moment Sojourners seems more indifferent than hostile to the legacy of Niebuhr. It's as if the urgency of their task doesn't allow time for them to carry around intellectual-theological baggage from the tradition. Beginning in small places, they are about the business of transforming the world with activist Christians as instruments of social and political justice.

Theological Naysayers

If Niebuhr is attractive as a tough-minded political realist, he is insufficiently orthodox for some Protestant Christian theologians and ethicists. Just as in his lifetime, Niebuhr continues to have formidable and outspoken Christian opponents. His most vociferous critic, the prolific Duke University theologian and ethicist Stanley Hauerwas, maintains that Niebuhr sold out the Christian faith to the interests of the world.[9] For such Christian voices, it isn't at all idiotic (in Arthur Schlesinger's words) for agnostics and secularists to admire Niebuhr's politics. The strong version of this criticism is that Niebuhr is only marginally related to the Christian faith in the first place. Hauerwas's 2001 Gifford Lectures in Scotland, *With the Grain of the Universe: The Church's Witness and Natural Theology* (2001), treat William James, Reinhold Niebuhr, and Karl Barth. The story line of this book is too vast to be rehearsed in detail. The book is, however, a sustained effort to argue that Niebuhr is a religious naturalist in the manner of William James, whose teaching falls far short of the "truthful language about God" set forth by the Swiss German twentieth-century theologian Karl Barth. In the eyes of Hauerwas, ever a polemicist and "Christian Contrarian," Niebuhr has just made too much peace with the world.[10] Having taught at the University of Notre Dame and, more recently, at Duke University, Hauerwas has virtually recast the map for thinking about Christian ethics as the discipline comes to bear upon the world. His differences with Niebuhr are severe, his criticism harsh. As a theological ethicist (his preferred self-designation), Hauerwas argues for a fundamentally different orientation to thinking about basic Christian issues.

Put more pointedly, Stanley Hauerwas is a Niebuhr apostate, who has spent the bulk of his career trying to distance himself from his early mentor. In *A Better Hope,* Hauerwas writes:

> Given my critical relation to Reinhold Niebuhr, some may find it odd I think it so important to maintain his significance, but such a view fails to appreciate that criticism is finally the deepest form of appreciation. I can only think the way I think because Reinhold Niebuhr made such important mistakes.[11]

His stance vis-à-vis Niebuhr reminds us of the literary critic Harold Bloom's *The Anxiety of Influence* (1973), which famously puts forth his theory of strong poets who turn, twist, and redirect the teaching of a preceding writer, thus emulating while rejecting the original master.[12] No one would wish to doubt that Stanley Hauerwas is a "strong poet." His restless temperament, prodigious energy, and prolific ability to address issues remind us that the Texan, like the son of German immigrants, is a force to be reckoned with.

A rehearsal of the salient points of Hauerwas's teaching sheds light on his movement as well as (in rejoinder) on the work of Niebuhr that I've been describing. Originally schooled at Yale Divinity School in the traditions of both Niebuhrs, Hauerwas began to doubt the adequacy of Niebuhr's theology when, teaching at the University of Notre Dame, he discovered John Howard Yoder's powerful Mennonite view of Jesus in *The Politics of Jesus.*[13] Writing from the perspective of a peace tradition, Yoder argues that the witness and Cross of Jesus have direct implications for radical Christian discipleship.

> The believer's cross is no longer any and every kind of suffering, sickness, or tension, the bearing of which is demanded. The believer's cross must be like his Lord's, the price of his social nonconformity. It is not, like sickness or catastrophe, an inexplicable, unpredictable suffering; it is the end of a path freely chosen after counting the cost. It is not, like Luther's or Thomas Müntzer's or Zinzendorf's or Kierkegaard's cross or *Anfechtung,* an inward wrestling of the sensitive soul with self and sin; it is the social reality of representing in an unwilling world the Order to come.[14]

The Jesus of Yoder and of Hauerwas calls his followers to direct action in modeling the pure self-sacrificial love in the world. Precisely the features of the Sermon on the Mount that Niebuhr once called an "impossible possibility" are put front and center as a scandal to the world.

To Hauerwas, Niebuhr is a pragmatist on the model of William James, who uses Christian symbols and language to underwrite a political agenda. Hauerwas's remarks on Niebuhr, like his other opinions, are deliberately cloaked in provocative language. His pacifism asserts itself with defiance against the world.[15] For Hauerwas, who pursues a theological ethics that focuses on personal virtue and character, the church constitutes the primary community for the practice of Christian discipleship. In contrast, Niebuhr is believed to be driven by pragmatic ends, takes the world of American politics as his community, and lacks a sense of the church as a God-given community. As an outspoken Christian pacifist who decries any sort of compromise with governing authority, Hauerwas holds that Niebuhr's endorsement of Christian symbols rests on a naturalistic, more than a theological, orientation. If Niebuhr is a theist, his is a "pale theism" that posits deity only in the sense of William James's yearning for "something more" in nature.[16] The criticism of Niebuhr from the side of a more theocentric and traditional orientation of faith elaborates certain of the issues for which Richard Niebuhr had also criticized his brother.[17] Yet there is irony in the fact that Hauerwas's vociferous stance vis-à-vis Niebuhr emulates its target by positioning himself as public theologian and theological polemicist against a sellout of the church to liberal progressivist social values.

At a time when pundits and opinion-makers are rediscovering Niebuhr's political relevance, his theological critics see him as having sold out the Christian message of love to the interests of political realism. In addition to the ambiguous reception of *Sojourners* "progressive Christianity" and the anti-Niebuhr fury of Stanley Hauerwas, other present-day Niebuhr critics are pursuing a movement called "radical orthodoxy" in Britain, with followers in the United States. Best exemplified by John Milbank of Cambridge University, a dominant line of criticism holds with Hauerwas that Niebuhr's theology is too worldly.[18] If Stanley Hauerwas is attempting to awaken a sense of Christian discipleship beyond Niebuhr, the proponents of radical orthodoxy believe that the wicked turning point in the history of theology began further back, with Duns Scotus in the Middle Ages.[19] In basic sympathy with Hauerwas's theology, their "sensibility" leads them to a far greater effort to rewrite the history of theology leading up to their project in what they depict as a postsecular, postmodern world. Technical articles and books seek to expose Reinhold Niebuhr as a Stoic in Christian disguise and as a purely political pragmatist and religious naturalist. Like Hauerwas, but on a broader historical-theological plane, radical orthodoxy writers focus on the independence of a God-given church and its majesty as the instrument of human salvation in the world. On this view Niebuhr's relative disinterest in doctrinal teaching (the dogma of Christ as human and divine, the three persons of the Trinity, or the nature of the resurrected Christ) contributes to an impression of worldliness. Since government of any kind is suspect, the way to have an impact on the world with integrity is through the loving community of the church. Yet for Niebuhr an approach that takes the church as a divine agent without remainder places a huge moral and metaphysical burden on a human institution. All human institutions, perhaps especially the bearers of religion, must be viewed in a critical perspective. The prophets of Israel never endorsed the priestly functionaries of the temple carte blanche. Along with St. Paul and the sixteenth-century Protestant Reformers, Niebuhr viewed the church as "treasure in earthen vessels."

On War, Peace, and Hauerwas

To close students of Niebuhr's legacy it's obvious that concurrently with the political revival of Niebuhr during the Iraq war, an intra-Christian tussle was unfolding over the meaning of Niebuhr's legacy. Just as the Iraq war brought new attention to *The Irony of American History,* it also provoked Christian writers on war and peace—topics that invariably brought them back to Niebuhr. Readers of the prominent journal on religion and politics, *First Things: A Journal of Religion, Culture, and Public Life* (edited by the late Richard John Neuhaus), might have guessed that Niebuhr was in trouble when onetime Niebuhr pupil and Protestant theologian Gabriel Fackre published a 2002 article, "Was Reinhold Niebuhr a Christian?"[20] In answering with a resounding affirmative, Fackre's article signaled the theological affinity of a journal that had long learned from Niebuhr.[21] Theological suspicion of and disaffection with Niebuhr proceeded apace with his popularity among political pundits. In fact, Fackre's defense of Niebuhr as a Christian in the pages of *First Things* followed turmoil within the editorial ranks of the journal over its backing of the invasion of Afghanistan following the September 11, 2001 attacks.

When *First Things* published its editorial in defense of the war in Afghanistan ("In Time of War," December 2001), its longtime contributing editor, Stanley Hauerwas, resigned in protest.[22] Although the imperialism debate with George W. Bush's presidency focused on the March 2003 invasion of Iraq, a prior moral question was posed for Niebuhrians concerning the initial invasion of Afghanistan. Addressing that issue, University of Chicago political philosopher Jean Bethke Elshtain published *Just War on Terror: The Burden of American Power in a Violent World.*[23] Elshtain invoked just war doctrine, especially that of retaliatory action, in defense of the invasion and drew upon Niebuhr and Paul Tillich in defense of her position. Her reason for writing the book was that petitions of Catholic bishops and other Christian groups urged no overt military response to the attacks of September 11, 2001. By the time it appeared in 2003, Elshtain's book was read and understood as in defense of the March invasion of Iraq, and she was powerfully taken to task for endorsing the Bush war on terror.[24]

The point here is simply to show that Christian writers, like their secular counterparts, have legitimate, and often painful, differences in matters of war and peace. As a pacifist and member of the Fellowship of Reconciliation prior to 1940, Niebuhr knew the power of the tradition in which Stanley Hauerwas stands. His rejection of that position was not undertaken casually. Contrary to some of his critics, Niebuhr did not use just war theory in any strict sense in coming to his view that war might sometimes be necessary. He was generally wary of the natural law moral traditions of Catholicism that are used to justify acts of war. In his view even a justifiable war cannot obscure its tragic nature through intellectual justification, even if it meets the criteria of being retaliatory, proportional, and has prospects for a good outcome. Niebuhr believed that the stakes involved in fighting a just war had been heightened, though not eliminated, in the nuclear age: "Because the ultimate consequences of atomic warfare cannot be measured, only the most imperative demands of justice have a clear sanction." He continued:

> For this reason, the occasions to which the concept of the just war can be rightly applied have become highly restricted. A war to defend the victims of wanton aggression, where the demands of justice join the demands of order, is today the clearest case of a just war. But where the immediate claims of order and justice conflict, as in a war initiated to secure freedom for the oppressed, the case is now much less clear. The claims of justice are no less. But because contemporary war places so many moral values in incalculable jeopardy, the immediate claims of order have become much greater. Although oppression was never more abhorrent to the Christian conscience or more dangerous to the longer-range prospects of peace than today, the concept of a just war does not provide moral justification for initiating a war of incalculable consequences to end such oppression.[25]

It is not surprising if there is ongoing disagreement among Christians on issues of war and peace.

Intra-Christian debates regarding Niebuhr's teaching are instructive. Since his criticism is so prominent, Stanley Hauerwas's differences with

Niebuhr, beginning with the charge that Niebuhr has, in effect, sold out the church to the world deserve a response.[26] Hauerwas's general charge breaks down into several distinct parts, including the view that Niebuhr (a) understands theology in a human or naturalistic ("Jamesian") manner that begins and ends with human nature, while neglecting aspects of Christian teaching that are needed for the work of discipleship, (b) lacks a robust sense of the church as a God-given institution that can rival and stand over against the political arena, and (c) acknowledges the radicality of Jesus's self-sacrificial love, but finds it inapplicable to the fallen and sinful world. For the most part Hauerwas (sometimes begrudgingly) acknowledges that Niebuhr was a practicing Christian believer and lived an exemplary life. But he just doesn't think that Niebuhr's ethics are anchored theologically within the Christian tradition.

A brief rejoinder to Hauerwas's main concerns must include a number of considerations. First, the account I am giving of Niebuhr has not disguised the fact that his greatest theological contribution is based upon the analysis of human nature. The key question is whether the anthropology is significantly identifiable as Christian. Like countless other convinced and creative Christian minds, including biblical writers in the New Testament, Niebuhr gives the Gospel message his own slant. Hauerwas in fact does the same via John Howard Yoder. If the problem is that Niebuhr doesn't touch all the bases and is thus one-sided, the same charge reflects back on Hauerwas. Neither Niebuhr nor Hauerwas provides a systematic account of the whole of theology. We've seen how Niebuhr, as a contextual writer, draws from a range of biblical teaching that includes the Old Testament prophets, the Psalms, the teachings of St. Paul, and subsequent theologians. Getting a theology started, like taking a position in politics, requires an act of hermeneutical judgment. The chief question is whether Niebuhr's anthropology is in fact a Christian anthropology, and there is every reason to believe that it is. As noted in chapter 3, Niebuhr deliberately appropriates the teaching of St. Paul, Augustine, and Kierkegaard regarding the foibles of sinful humanity, and how repentance opens the door to gracious renewal through the forgiveness of a transcendent, mysterious deity. That's the anthropology that transformed the teaching of classical Greek and Roman antiquity. If the world of politics and secular pundits recognize merit in the diagnosis, so much the better for Christian thought.

Second, it is true that Niebuhr does not develop a full-scale doctrine of the church, what theologians call "ecclesiology." The reasons behind that are fairly straightforward. Niebuhr was at once a thoroughgoing man of the church as preacher, writer, ecumenical activist, and organizer. At the same time, he was a great critic of the church as he came to experience it in his day. His formative years were all shaped in the immigrant German Synod, which became the Evangelical and Reformed Church (combining Lutheranism and Calvinism from northern Germany), and eventually merged with the Congregationalists to form the United Church of Christ, the denomination now shared with Obama. His years between World Wars I and II were spent in the deepest counsels of the ecumenical movement as it struggled first with the European economic crises and then for an appropriate Christian strategy against Hitler. When Harvard president James B. Conant offered him an interdisciplinary university professorship in 1942, Niebuhr chose to stay with the "specifically Christian foundation" of Union Theological Seminary. In that sense, Niebuhr saw himself as a servant of the church, despite the fact that he never wrote a treatise called *De ecclesia* ("On the Church"). If having a high doctrine of the church is the litmus test for being a significant Christian, the test will exclude not just Reinhold Niebuhr, but also St. Francis and Dr. Martin Luther King. Niebuhr's *Essays in Applied Christianity* includes a large number of provocative essays on liturgy, church leadership, the relative strengths of Catholicism and Protestantism, and the Christian church in times of crisis.

Niebuhr's ministerial gifts and choices differ from those of Hauerwas, just as they do from the more local, grassroots orientation of Sojourners and other Christian activists. But his was a powerful and effective practice of ministerial gifts, and there's no reason to think that all Christian practices should follow the same formulae. Niebuhr's collected essays on applied Christianity talk repeatedly about the weaknesses of the church and call for its renewal by taking the moral life seriously. His program may not be identical with Hauerwas's, but it scarcely stands on the margins of Christianity.

Third, the Cross of Jesus looms large over all of Niebuhr's work. For him it symbolizes the fractured and broken nature of our lives. Hauerwas's version of the Christian life is one of challenging others by protesting the violence rampant at all levels of life in the world. That is thoroughly honorable, as far as it goes. But Niebuhr's way of following Jesus takes him not only as model of behavior but also as the supreme teacher who calls us to account when we have fallen short of the mark. Niebuhr views the meaning of Jesus through the prophets of Israel and teachings of St. Paul. His call for contrition and repentance and the value he puts on forgiveness as the final form of love draw from a central tradition of Christian faith. Strangely enough, Niebuhr is like Hauerwas in wanting to stress the building of human character; to that end he calls for us to come to grips with hypocrisy in all its forms.

In the end, I do not think any of what I write will be convincing to Stanley Hauerwas or to his followers. Nor does that probably matter. On my view, the real difference between Hauerwas and Niebuhr resides elsewhere, and consists in the fact that Niebuhr is far more aware of the contingencies of history and of historical traditions than is Hauerwas. His account of the role of irony in self-judgment and the dramas of history has never been surpassed. Niebuhr's Christianity aims at being in dialogue with the world and accepting the challenges that the world presents to a religious tradition. He apparently knew, as did Jesus of Nazareth, that persons outside of officially religious circles (harlots, tax collectors, sinners) were worth engaging. Hauerwas rightly wants to resist being seen as "sectarian," a label that is no more useful than calling Niebuhr a "dualist." For Niebuhr, human sin begins with the individual self and extends from there; as an Augustinian he holds that even the Christian church is not pure, but a "mixed body" of sinners and saints. Of course, Hauerwas wants to resist Niebuhr's charge of sometimes having to choose between moral purity and acting responsibly in society. When Niebuhr makes that point, he does so in full knowledge that actions taken will invariably leave us with an uneasy conscience, whether we are pacifists or whether we see the need for legitimate nonviolent (or even directly violent) coercion.

Finally, consider the following remarks of Stanley Hauerwas on politics and the Obama election. In a September 2008 interview with the *Other Journal.Com*, Hauerwas states:

> People forget that elections are not democracy. Elections are only the means to try to occasion the debates necessary for the discovery of goods in common that are impossible to be discovered without the debates. Elections themselves can be very coercive practices in which the majority gets to tell the minority what to do. So I think that the overestimation of elections as the defining mark of democracy, and how you even begin to think about democracy, is one of the things I would want to warn Christians about in this time. I will probably vote this time, but I don't always do so.[27]

In the next paragraph Hauerwas adds that "I don't regard national elections as politics; it's entertainment." Of course, there are times, especially during an election campaign, when the chatter of national politics fills the air with so many lies that one must scream simply to keep sane. But the paragraph cited betrays such a rudimentary grasp of democratic political theory as to make democracy seem like a matter of jest. It's easy to enjoy the luxury of religious freedom, if you already live where it is sustained. Cynicism toward the world is far greater on the part of Hauerwas than on the side of a tough-minded Niebuhrian. Lest we think the above quote is a slip of the tongue, followers of Niebuhr's legacy need to be aware that the view of not voting on Christian grounds has a wider following in some Christian circles, though not those connected with Sojourners.[28] If doubt remains on whether the voice of Niebuhr is still needed in the Christian world and the political world, Stanley Hauerwas has helped to make that case. Niebuhr's understanding of sin and human pretension is compelling on the point that we must occasionally choose between being pure and being responsible. Being morally pure is the greatest self-delusion of all, whether on Christian or any other grounds.

The Perils of a Politicized Faith

We've seen that Niebuhr's Christian detractors think he has an insufficient appreciation of the centrality of the church as institution or in Pauline language as "the body of Christ." The point is central to our day when many of us legitimately question institutional religion in general, the roles of churches, synagogues, and mosques in the U. S. polity, or the forms of radical Islam on the world stage. My defense of Niebuhr as a man of the church is not inconsistent with his high level of suspicion of the institutional church with its "admixtures of the grace of Christ and the pride of nations and cultures." The institutional church is needed to mediate divine grace through its teachings and sacraments. But the truly universal church is "the community of saints, known and unknown, among whom life is constantly transformed because it is always under the divine word."[29]

Niebuhr's biblical faith made him suspicious of all that is mortal. That suspicion was reinforced by two historical-biographical factors: his experiences as a pastor beginning in the 1920s, and the subsequent rise of Nazi and Communist states, each driven by a quasi-religious ideology. First, as a pastor Niebuhr found the Protestant churches all too frequently unwilling to recognize and confront the social disarray and injustice around them. He felt as if the churches were unwilling to act because they had such difficulty agreeing on what was worth doing that was consistent with the love of Christ. A 1948 essay, "Can the Churches Give a 'Moral Lead'?," states:

> There are undoubtedly some basic moral convictions, transcending political and strategic problems, to which all Christians are committed. There are others to which they ought to be committed, though they are not. The church cannot afford to deal merely in vague generalities because it lacks unanimous convictions on the level of political strategy. It remains a fact, nevertheless, that the church is divided by every partisan interest of geographic or racial, economic or political origin. That fact alone is a proof that the sanctity of the church does not consist in the goodness of its members but in the holiness of its Lord.[30]

Second, on the larger stage of history, the rise of Nazism in the native Germany of his family tradition, showed the complete dominance of church life by the state, including a taking over of ritual and sacred functions. Facing the idolatrous Nazi state of Hitler, Niebuhr wrote in 1940, "It is a tragic world, troubled not by finiteness so much as by 'false eternals' and false absolutes, and expressing the pride of these false absolutes even in the highest reaches of its spirituality."[31] In citing these words, we are highlighting the theological counterpart of his arguments against national arrogance and imperialism that are touched on at various points in this book.

Niebuhr's theology, together with his life experience, taught him that religious institutions are prone to all the foibles of human life. Yet the stakes are even higher, since religious institutions so often cloak their deeds and pronouncements in a sacred aura, as if intended by God. Niebuhr agrees with the view of his nineteenth-century predecessor Friedrich Schleiermacher that religion never appears "in a pure state."[32] But neither of them took this as a reason to abandon the church. Niebuhr knew that by its nature religion makes absolute claims that arise from faith in God and instill courage in believers. That holds for the Christian Church, just as it does for other major faiths. But it does mean that religion and its institutions are among the potentially dangerous pursuits of humankind.

As a cover for our anxiety religion potentially feeds "true belief" and fanaticism. Faced with that reality, developing a self-critical, reflective faith is the best antidote for idolatrous views of self, society, or the state. Proper religious faith, for Niebuhr, views both communities of faith and political life from a transcendent standard of morality. Like Luther, looking at the sixteenth-century Roman Catholic Church, Niebuhr rests the case for religion on a radically transcendent sense of deity, a God who cannot be manipulated by humans, whether in politics or in religious institutions. For Niebuhr, the first of the Ten Commandments ("You shall have no other

Gods before me, Exod. 20: 2–3") stands before all the others. It is also very likely the most frequently violated.

Hence Christian belief rests upon symbolic (nonliteral) speech, celebrated in liturgical rituals that evoke a rich history. His sense of radical transcendence draws mainly from Judaism and Christianity but has analogies with other religions. A degree of self-doubt remains in place, even at the heart of Christian faith. From the 1948 essay just cited:

> The Christian faith gives us no warrant to lift ourselves above the world's perplexities and to seek or to claim absolute validity for the stand we take. It does, however, encourage us to the charity, which is born of humility and contrition. This is not a 'clear moral lead' but a clear religious insight into the fragmentary character of all human morality, including the virtue of the saints and the political pronouncement of churches. . . . If we claim to possess overtly what remains hidden, we turn the mercy of Christ into an inhuman fanaticism.[33]

However imperfect, the church is a community that carries forth the message of selfless love, while seeking proximate solutions to the problem of justice.

Of course, it is a truism of our society today that religion is easily linked to violence. That is presumably what moves some Christians to become pacifists and Christopher Hitchens to believe that religion is incompatible with civilization. Consider the words of Catholic Monsignor Lorenzo Albacete (PBS Frontline show *Faith and Doubt at Ground Zero*), an eyewitness to the 9/11 destruction of Manhattan's twin towers.

> From the first moment I looked into that explosion of horror I knew it. I knew it before anything was said. I recognized an old companion. I recognized religion. The same fire, energy, and passionate instinct that motivates religious people to do great things is the same one that brought all that destruction. . . . There is no more destructive force on the face of this earth than a religious passion.

The association of religion with power and violence is so strong that the *New York Times* bureau chief in Baghdad, John Burns, could soberly describe the bombing of Baghdad on the early morning of March 20, 2003, as a "biblical experience," adding that

> even those reporters who are not believers were reaching for words that are associated with the powers of God as we saw cruise missiles hit and explode. It was like the most powerful fireworks display you've ever seen magnified a thousand times.

Niebuhr's Christian realism acknowledges the power as well as the dangers inherent in a religious faith. The lessons taught by the Nazis' utter ruin of his ancestral home of Germany and threat to world civilization—in the name of an Aryan God—were never lost on Niebuhr. As the most egregious form of idolatry, religious nationalism must be resisted through rational criticism, proportional direct action, and a resolute defense of democratic principles.

For Niebuhr, religion has a role in the public square, so long as religious freedom for all persons is protected. Separation of church and state preserves the robustness of our democracy. Barack Obama's view of how faith relates to politics in a multicultural, pluralistic society echoes Niebuhr. As Obama puts the case in *The Audacity of Hope,* if we assume we "only had Christians within our borders, whose Christianity would we teach in the schools? James Dobson's or Al Sharpton's?" He notes further that "secularists are wrong when they ask believers to leave their religion at the door before entering the public square," and that "the majority of great reformers in American history—not only were motivated by faith but repeatedly used religious language to argue their causes."[34] But this works, for Obama and for Niebuhr, only when religious values connect with larger moral aims.

> What our deliberative, pluralistic democracy does demand is that the religiously motivated translate their concerns into universal, rather than religion-specific, values. It requires that their proposals be subject to argument, and amenable to reason. If I am opposed to abortion for religious reasons, but seek to pass a law banning the practice, I cannot simply point to the teachings of my church. I have to explain why abortion violates some principle that is accessible to people of all faiths, including those with no faith at all.[35]

Like Niebuhr, Obama feels a need to transfer the specific grounds for Christian action into more universal language for the sake of the larger community. On these issues Niebuhr is as critical-minded toward religion as he is toward politics.

For a theological critic like Stanley Hauerwas "Constantinianism" signifies the long history of cozy relations between Altar and Crown that began early in the fourth century.[36] The legitimate fear is that Christian truth will accommodate and capitulate to cultural values. But it remains debatable when, whether, and where such capitulations take place. Since Christianity is not culturally self-contained, it invariably shares in some fashion with the larger culture. Niebuhr's critics' assault on the values of the eighteenth-century Enlightenment as a sellout of proper Christian faith to generalized morality seems ill-conceived, just as does the assault on Niebuhr's theology for viewing traditional religious language as symbolic. His saying that we should "take myth seriously but not literally" arises from awareness that the human heart seeks false security and tends to absolutize. In taking the long, prophetic view of religion and human history, Niebuhr refuses to defend religious faith by appealing to forms of supernaturalism. Being committed to the position that human goodness is never pure has as its corollary an extraordinarily rich view of divine mercy and grace. Niebuhr is too aware of human ambiguity to speak glibly about the activity of God working among us. When we lack an ability to discern "the signs of the times," this is due "not to a defect of the mind in calculating the course of history but to a corruption of the heart, which introduced the confusion of selfish pride into the estimate of historical events."[37] Whatever happens in the near term, he is confident that the culmination of history will be full of grace and divine forgiveness, a culmination that lies beyond history. Such a mythic picture cannot be verified. When it is espoused in faith, it projects a morally consistent view of the human story that enables us to live meaningfully amid the highs and lows of everyday existence.

Unlike literalist Christians, Niebuhr is wary of knee-jerk efforts to directly identify events as acts of God, whether 9/11 as punishment for abortion and lesbianism (Pat Robertson, Jerry Falwell)[38] or the politicized evangelical Christians who urge Israeli militancy against Palestinians in order to hasten the rapture of the end time. A sense of God's presence, for Niebuhr, is felt prayerfully, not on the basis of casual disclosure. If this separates him from traditionalists in religion who wish to witness to God in all their deeds, it is a price Niebuhr is willing to pay. This is why he endorses the view that theological language must be symbolic and that myth "must be taken seriously but not literally." To speak literally of what is beyond human understanding easily crosses over to idolatry, which clings to its object out of a false sense of security. Rather than being diminished, the classical Christian teachings on death and resurrection are not less powerful when viewed symbolically. Symbols, myths, and metaphors are real, and reach into everyday existence. Life often does seem like a perpetual Good Friday in which goodness loses out and innocent suffering stands before our eyes. But the intimations of deity in the surprises of our lives, acts of selfless love and beneficence within the church and among family, friends, or even strangers, convey the reality of an Easter faith.

Secular admirers of his politics need not feel cut off from or alienated by the Christian origination and foundation of Niebuhr's teaching. To the apparent consternation of some of his theological critics, his Christian anthropology intersects with common human experience. His way of framing the issues of religion speaks at once to those within and to those outside of formal religious practices. Similarly, his theological admirers—possibly readers of Marilynne Robinson's prize-winning novel *Gilead,* whose narrator, John Ames, still believes in sin—need not shrink from endorsing his political realism. For Niebuhr religion and politics address the same unfathomable mystery that stands behind all of life and human creativity. Faith in God as "creator and Lord of all" undergirds his theological perspective, even where this affirmation transcends human understanding. The fact that humans are finite and limited has serious implications for our ability to grasp the ways of the Almighty.

7

LIVING WITH NIEBUHR'S LEGACY

We are not facing a new spiritual crisis: this is the same old crisis in a new form. Living in history, living in full, always offers as much despair as hope, as much danger as possibility.

Niebuhr's daughter, Elisabeth Sifton, in *The Serenity Prayer: Faith and Politics in Times of Peace and War* (New York / London: W. W. Norton & Company, 2003)

"Will Rogers speaks greater truths than more pretentious prophets dare to utter," declared Professor Reinhold Niebuhr in his first sermon as a member of the Faculty of Union Theological Seminary yesterday morning in the seminary chapel, Broadway at 120th Street.

From the *New York Times* (November 19, 1928)

The task of pondering the impact of Niebuhr on our time and place has shaped the present inquiry. Figuring out what more needs to be said is not an easy task. In 1986 Robert McAfee Brown declined to write an article for the *Christian Century* under the title "Why I am Still a Niebuhrian." That was probably a wise choice, even if the adjective is occasionally useful. In fact, Niebuhr's thought cannot be reduced to a single word or label, even one involving his own name.

From the outset we have been struck by Niebuhr's interest "in the defense and justification of the Christian faith in a secular age."[1] Taking on that task placed him directly amid the tensions of modernity. Confusion continues to reign over whether Niebuhr is a religious or a secular thinker, even if putting matters that way rests on a set of inherited traditions. In fact the assumption of a firm division between secularity and religion is increasingly called into question. The distinction was unknown to the prophets of Israel, who inform Niebuhr's perspective. For them the Creator God informs all that exists, even when the deity remains hidden and unrecognized.

As a writer Niebuhr brings past thinkers into a vast network of illuminating ideas, sorting and sifting along the way. Typically he defends middle ground against extremes, as in his attacks on overly consistent mental and biological accounts of human nature. His persistent voice can be polemical. In Niebuhr's hands irony and satire are used with a generosity of spirit in which the standard of judgment reflects back on the critic's own life. As he occasionally put it in a riff on St. Paul's First Corinthians letter, "There's a difference between being a 'fool for Christ' and 'a plain damn fool.'" Tolerance of foolishness is not a Christian virtue. There's nothing in the Bible that says Christians must be naive in viewing the world and the life around them.

Against Popular Tides

It may give Barack Obama pause if he realizes that throughout his life Niebuhr was a tough critic of cozy relationships between clergy and politicians, especially at the top. He was especially harsh on Billy Graham, the permanent counselor to occupants of the oval office.[2] His 1969 piece, "The King's Chapel and the King's Court," attacks Richard Nixon's establishment of private worship services that turned the East Room of the White House into a sanctuary. The practice, Niebuhr argues, offends against the nonestablishment clause of the first article of the Bill of Rights. Against such comfortable religiosity Niebuhr calls on words of the eighth-century prophet Amos, who spoke of the rulers of Israel "who trample upon the needy, and bring the poor of the land to an end . . ." (Amos 8:4). Accordingly, Niebuhr sharply criticizes the piety of prayer breakfasts and the religiosity that surrounds inaugurations and other affairs of state.[3]

It is not customary to find theologians on presidential reading lists.[4] So it was probably a surprise to learn that Barack Obama lists Niebuhr as his favorite philosopher. The strand of Christian theology that teaches the fallenness of the world has bracing lessons for the leader of a nation in a time of crisis. An anecdote involving FDR is worth noting. Preceding chapters have drawn parallels between Niebuhr's analysis of human nature and the Danish philosopher Søren Kierkegaard. That Franklin Delano Roosevelt knew something of Kierkegaard on human sin is a little known fact. Frances Perkins, head of the War Labor Board, reports in her memoir that FDR encouraged her to read Kierkegaard. "It will teach you about the Nazis," the president said, continuing:

> Kierkegaard explains the Nazis to me as nothing else ever has. I have never been able to make out why people who are obviously human beings could behave like that. They are human, yet they behave like demons. Kierkegaard gives you an understanding of what it is in man that makes it possible for these Germans to be so evil.[5]

FDR refused to view the world as a Manichean contest between good and evil. That fourth-century struggle, fought in the time of Augustine, was a lesson of history that shaped Niebuhr's thought. Not just FDR but his historian, Arthur Schlesinger, Jr., though an agnostic, found insight into original sin a sure guide to the depravity of the death camps. What makes Niebuhr's voice compelling is his ability to take a stand on the age-old struggles of the human race. It seems reasonable to imagine that FDR was a more judicious and wiser opponent of Nazi Germany for refusing to demonize the German people.

Despite the Niebuhr revival among political writers and pundits, his teaching goes against the grain of American culture, just as it did in his lifetime. Acknowledging this fact reminds us of the adage that history always repeats itself, but never in the same way. His view of the human will's weakness is tough to swallow, even when daily headlines of an America in crisis sustain the diagnosis. Many, if not most, Americans are incorrigible optimists, as if "positive thinking" were our national creed. A tide of opposition to Niebuhr prevails, alongside the revival of interest in his work.

Norman Vincent Peale's *The Power of Positive Thinking* (1952), published in the same year as *The Irony of American History,* was a bestseller for decades. Along with the evangelist Billy Graham, Peale was the best-known clergyman of his day, known to millions of Americans. Today a successor movement called "positive psychology" exists among research psychologists. It draws data from neural science to show that altruistic impulses and caring for others contributes to health, well-being, and longevity. One popular account, Sonja Lyubomirsky's *The How of Happiness: A Scientific Approach to Getting the Life You Want* (Penguin Press, 2007), claims that up to 40 percent of our level of happiness is within our power to change.[6] When asked whether the principles of "positive psychology" apply to political questions, practitioners of the movement have little to say. Individual well-being proceeds on its own track, more or less oblivious to political life. Celebrity inspirational speakers with a Peale-like "positive thinking" message regularly stalk the convention centers and promise success, usually meaning higher paying jobs, for attendees. Popular currents of American thought, such as the purported link between prosperity and virtue, remain prominent. The refrain that "Peale has now become backed by science" is heard in some quarters. The novelty lies not in the message but in new marketing and media techniques that promise to guide others to personal success.

The desire to "feel good" about our human prospects has scarcely abated since Niebuhr's day. It's fed through the marketing of celebrity-endorsed success seminars and through the prestige of science. Consider this case in point: the invitation and leading question that publisher John Brockman put to contributors to the recent anthology *What are You Optimistic About? Today's Leading Thinkers on Why Things are Good and Getting Better* (2007).

> As an activity, as a state of mind, science is fundamentally optimistic. Science figures out how things work and thus can make them work better. Much of the news is either good news or news that can be made good, thanks to ever deepening knowledge and ever more efficient and powerful tools and techniques. Science, on its frontiers, poses more and ever better questions, ever better put. What are you optimistic about? Why? Surprise us![7]

In response, some 150 distinguished natural and social scientists, linguists, psychologists, and computer experts dutifully reassure us that the future will be better than the past. Philosopher Daniel C. Dennett writes on "The Evaporation of the Powerful Mystique of Religion," psychologist Steven Pinker on "The Decline of Violence," and biologist Richard Dawkins, author of *The God Delusion* (2006), expresses optimism that the theories of physics and biology "will furnish a totally satisfying naturalistic explanation for the existence of the universe and everything that's in it, including ourselves."[8] The contributions call to mind the remarks about "political infantilism" that Niebuhr once made about a nameless physician friend, under the heading "The Specialist": "His intelligence is exhausted in the field of his specialization."[9] Optimism as ideology leads to as many excesses as pessimism. In their zeal to be positive about the future the writers fail to grapple adequately with the brokenness of the global community with respect to extremes of poverty, systemic violence, world hunger, lack of educational opportunity, economic well-being, and issues of basic health.

New patterns of popular Christianity project an optimistic Christianity, the religious counterpart to the "scientific faith" in the future. Rather than cultivate a sense of history, such religious groups minimize their ties to the

Christian past. By comparison the denominational churches of Niebuhr's day seem staid and remote. Today the upbeat language, music, and marketing strategies of megachurches and other religious communities are taking over much of suburban America. The extent to which they are, in Niebuhr's words, "vulgarized" forms of religion with "vaudeville appeal" is subject to debate.[10] As self-described mission-based, grassroots communities, emerging churches are departing from the supply and demand marketing orientation and "needs meeting" strategies of the megachurches. Often they seek direct Christian engagement with the world. At a time when religion is associated with violence, the language of spirituality is co-opted for use in the worlds of business and commerce, as in the recently launched *Journal of Management, Spirituality and Religion* (Routledge, 2009), which aims at adding spiritual practices, including meditation and Feng Shui, to the "mix of the life-work balance."

All of these trends and signs of the times should suffice to indicate the vast divide that separates Niebuhr's appropriation of Christian faith from popular American culture. If we have grown up thinking that being optimistic is itself a virtue, Niebuhr seems especially scandalous. His thought challenges us to confront ourselves and our society in more complex ways. He had the knack of standing against popular tides, even when earning the respect of his critics. If he ever does become wildly popular, we should suspect that his central message has been diluted.

Learning from the Christian Past

It may be a reflection of our impatience with history that we find it hard to place Niebuhr within the Christian tradition that he affirms. Historical texts and figures are often held at arm's length. It's easier to read present-day interpretations than to struggle through books written in the past and ponder their meaning for today. That attitude echoes our busy lives. We view historical texts as the province of professional historians, as if their authors lacked the concerns and issues that face us today. Yet classic religious texts, and not just those of the Bible, cry out to be revisited afresh by each age. That is true of Luther's *On the Freedom of a Christian,* just as it is of Saint Augustine's *Confessions.* A significant dip into a classic of Christian tradition can be illuminating and thrilling, challenge old beliefs, and stretch one's sense of self through an encounter with religious questions posed in a different time and place.

We can engage the Christian past in many ways: through study of the Bible, by reading classics of the tradition, and by pondering the sweep of Christian history. It's easy for me to say this—I've spent a career doing it—but it's much harder to put into practice. In *Why Study of the Past? The Quest for the Historical Church* (2005), Rowan Williams reminds us that most Christians have only a minimal sense of their own traditions. He calls for a greater sense of maturity in approaching the Christian past.[11] He writes that

> traditionalists sometimes miss the point because they don't expect to be surprised by the past; progressives miss the point because they don't expect to be interested or questioned by it. And in a cultural setting where a sensible understanding of history is not much encouraged, it isn't surprising if religious people can be as much at sea as anyone else in coming to terms with the past.[12]

Williams reminds us that the beliefs we have in our heads about Christianity, to stay with the case at hand, are so familiar that they feel quite natural. We take *our way* of viewing as normal, while rejecting *those of others*. Williams has a marvelous ability to write about a tradition that is constantly evolving to meet new situations. He knows whereof he speaks. As Archbishop of Canterbury, he heads a deeply troubled Anglican World Communion. His perspective on the power and capacity of a tradition to reach new contours provides hope for the life of faith in years that lie ahead.

The dilemma we face in trying to learn from the Christian past does not differ from that of any other encounter with history. Do we engage the past mainly for its own sake? Or do we try to plumb the past primarily to find meaning in the present? Do we want encyclopedic knowledge about Christianity or do we want a living faith that will assist us in facing the challenges of today? Modern inquiry is deeply aware of this tension between past and present. Today we know that any representation of the past, including this book about Reinhold Niebuhr, is based upon an encounter with work that was conceived under other circumstances in a different time and place. Interpreting the past requires us to be wary and bold at one and the same time. In the words of New Testament scholar Krister Stendahl, if we seek to replicate the past for its own sake we risk "archaizing" ourselves; we may feel tempted to play "Bibleland" and act as if we are exact contemporaries of Jesus. Conversely, if we overemphasis the present moment, we risk "modernizing" our subject matter; applied to the present case, we treat Niebuhr as if he were an exact contemporary.[13] Sometimes this strange task of trying to draw authentic meaning for today from the past is given the name "hermeneutics." The name appropriately derives from the Greek messenger god, Hermes, who flitted about the heavens conveying messages from the distant gods to mere mortals.

But such scholarly talk does not meet the practical needs of readers who may want to dip into Niebuhr more directly and decide for themselves about his relevance. Persons who have heard me speak about Niebuhr in teaching situations have made me aware of a need for practical guidance, not just more information. With that in mind several good options present themselves. For those who are computer-savvy, the NPR *Speaking of Faith* Web site "Moral Man and Immoral Society: Rediscovering Reinhold Niebuhr" offers a natural point of departure. It includes timely articles on Niebuhr, interviews with scholars and theologians about his legacy, several audio clips of his sermons and talks, and artifacts (photos and documents) illustrating his life that can be accessed interactively.[14] A reading of *The Irony of American History* might well be accompanied by reading through the sermons and prayers in the book *Justice and Mercy,* which much deserves its own reprinting. Taken together the two titles capture the political analyst who speaks on the world stage and the pastor who speaks to the troubled hearts of parishioners. More venturesome readers may want to pick up the original Niebuhr blockbuster and seminal work *Moral Man and Immoral Society.*[15] For those who want more of a sense of Niebuhr in his own time and place, Charles C. Brown's biography, *Niebuhr and His Age: Reinhold Niebuhr's Prophetic Role and Legacy,* combines theological as well as historical sophistication and points readers to a wide body of literature on all facets of Niebuhr's life and teaching.[16]

Armed with our own sense of Niebuhr, we are better prepared to encounter his interpreters. This book began with a road map of the current political interest in Niebuhr. The debate about American imperialism appropriately latches onto Niebuhr as an engaged, prophetic critic of American history and culture. Diplomatic historian Andrew J. Bacevich's book, *The Limits of Power,* justifiably attacks the folly of George W. Bush's Iraq adventurism and warns against its future repetition. The book's analysis extends its author's introduction to the new edition of *The Irony of American History* and offers a powerful indictment that legitimately draws from Niebuhr. *Limits of Power* appeared in 2008 at a time when a new American administration had been elected, and the Iraq War with its ongoing repercussions forms only one act in the complex drama now unfolding in

U.S. domestic as well as foreign policy. It's hard to be ironic and prophetic at one and the same time. Bacevich's approach to Niebuhr is badly needed and has immediate relevance. At the same time, such political treatments of Niebuhr lack a touch of his self-critical dimension that reflects universally on humanity gone awry as well as on the partialities of our historical judgments. The ironic and dispassionate Niebuhr is minimized in accounts of the political left, while a sense that his persistent moral energy should be disciplined by the lessons of history is exaggerated on the right.

In these pages I have been walking a fine line between approaching Niebuhr in his own time and place and suggesting his relevance for today. How to weigh past and present in such a project is a balancing act. By stating early on that Niebuhr's biography is backdrop for this account of his thought, I have emphasized the present and ongoing significance of Niebuhr more than what he meant for his immediate contemporaries. In the end, however, his thought cannot be separated from his biography. In earlier chapters I have drawn from the immediate Christian terrain that informed Niebuhr's teaching, including his reading habits and ways of incorporating the past in his own contemporary world. We've seen perennial resistance to his teaching, both in the past and today. I've stressed the ways that significant aspects of the teaching of St. Paul and Augustine and of Luther and Kierkegaard fed his theological imagination. We've also noted that Niebuhr's encounter with these thinkers within the tradition occurred in the midst of debates with towering contemporaries like John Dewey, Sidney Hook, Sigmund Freud, Paul Tillich, and others. Niebuhr's thought models a way of living with a sense of history as it affects one's own time and place. His persistent voice is rare, but it is hardly unprecedented. It's no small task to deepen one's insight through an encounter with the past. That is what I have attempted to do with this inquiry into Niebuhr's significance in today's world.

The process by which Niebuhr came to his set of views is not unique to a theologian. When confronted with novelty and shock, when things go horribly wrong, we try to square our perceptions with what is known. The process works this way in the worlds of scientific research and in literary detection. We first try to size up individual behavior or raise questions about groups of people. When adverse trends show up and standard answers fail, we may start to wonder about the makeup of humans as a whole. Thinking about our nature as humans is hard work; if we do it at all, we do it in fleeting moments, in a piecemeal fashion. Typically those who think about humanity broadly are philosophers or theologians; but they also may be novelists, poets, filmmakers, playwrights, social scientists, or biologists. They wonder why, under certain conditions, we behave in particular ways. Their ideas challenge received understandings of human behavior, including consciousness and the brain. They deal with questions of value, asking why we don't live up to our ideals, or why we have a need to be respected and loved by others. At their best such observers convey unusual and challenging insight into life's quandaries, based upon how they see our nature as humans.

Thinking about our uses of the Christian past can only be suggestive. The patterns through which we seek meaning in history cut in all directions, including the present study. In his own work, which draws so much from history, Niebuhr drew positive examples from intellectual history, while he debunked other strata of thought, such as the overconfidence of rationalism, whether ancient Greek or modern American. I make no secret of my belief that Niebuhr remains highly relevant as political thinker and as theologian. The Niebuhr I am concerned with touches on many fronts. I have been most concerned to show how his personal and political experience puts the Christian tradition's teaching on sinful humanity front and center. If we pre-filter Niebuhr too much, we miss the complex range of his legacy.

Knowing Oneself and the Christian Faith

As previously noted in these pages, I have attempted to trace the political teaching of Niebuhr to his Christian anthropology while suggesting the ongoing relevance of his thought. I want to ask whether Niebuhr can be appreciated on his own terms, even as he speaks to today's world. His teaching about our inevitable illusions and moral blindness is a tough pill to swallow. Is it possible for me, or for my nation, to live without the illusion of self-importance? Such questions haunt this inquiry and deserve a response. We need to remind ourselves of Niebuhr's complexity of mind, especially the fact that self-preoccupation makes us poor judges in our own cases. We are not evil so much as warped by pride or sloth that arises from the lack of equilibrium between mind, body, and will. As creatures we are in the natural order with our wants and desires; yet our human glory and that of science lie in our capacity to stand above ourselves to make new discoveries and to weigh moral choices, including the fate of the earth. Along with novelists and psychoanalysts, Niebuhr knows that dark secrets render good intentions ominous. Having a sense of history reminds us of our place in the larger scheme of things. A sense of humor and irony helps us get on with life, while self-effacing humility keeps us sane when we fall short of the mark. This sense of "knowing oneself" is crucial to the best of our literary and philosophical traditions. It lies at the heart of political realism. It also lies at the heart of the Christian faith in the form of repentance, the self-knowledge of contrition that prepares for the reality of divine forgiveness and unmerited new beginnings that the tradition names as grace.

Of course, for all of Niebuhr's appeal, there's natural resistance to his teaching. He is dismissed as pessimistic, cynical, and painting with too broad a brush. We have a pronounced desire to minimize or ignore what Niebuhr, along with Pascal and Hawthorne, sees as the sordid side of our nature. We do well to linger a bit more over the contested theme of Niebuhr on human sin. A friend of mine with a lifetime of experience teaching philosophy and ethics confirms the view of this book that "sin" is no longer a word in the active vocabulary of today's undergraduates, who even resist thinking that humans have a capacity to do evil. In turn, his mature adult students, who know the liturgical incantations about "sin," shrink back from attributing it to anyone they know.[17] It's apparently far easier to live with an easy conscience, while holding the daily headlines of war, greed, scandal, sexual abuse, and human depravity at a distance. Yet the yield of Niebuhr's legacy is that the tendencies toward a distorted sense of self that lead to such depravity lurk within each of us and surface with regularity, even if in less dramatic ways. No one should pretend that seeking moral self-knowledge is an easy task.

What follows, then, for our lives if we acknowledge both good and evil tendencies in ourselves, while knowing how difficult or impossible it is to judge such matters honestly? How can we live with such troubling incongruities? Recognizing evil within oneself or one's nation requires an act of truthful self-scrutiny and painful self-recognition. That task requires courage. Niebuhr's view of human nature also requires a sense of hope, not as wishful thinking, but as belief that the created order is good and that despite our shortcomings, life is worth living. As we've seen, this hard-won biblical truth was reclaimed in Christian antiquity against the Manichean worldview. Even St. Paul, often maligned in today's churches as the architect of original sin, acknowledges that we have a permanent sense of moral good in our minds.

Niebuhr's first published book, *Leaves from the Notebook of a Tamed Cynic* (1929), flirts with cynicism, but rejects it as empty. For a real cynic, like the ancient gnostics, life in the world is alien and meaningless. Unlike the Gnostic, who flees toward inwardness, the cynic mocks the world by (literally) dog-like public behavior. The self-description "tamed cynic" tells us that Niebuhr looked meaninglessness in the face, and decided against it.[18] But if he rejects cynicism's negativity, he also rejects the unshakable confidence of Stoicism that is bought at the price of detachment from worldly responsibility. We've seen how Epictetus, a first-century contemporary of St. Paul, urges us to avoid what lies beyond our control. For him the only things worth worrying about are mental. Epictetus achieves serenity by distancing himself from just the kind of responsible concern for others that is demanded by the Christian faith. The idea of human nature requiring a struggle of the whole self, and not just mental discipline, is more Pauline than Stoic. Christian insight into human vulnerability and the fickleness of the human will is irreconcilable with classical Stoicism.

Not the least part of Niebuhr's appeal lies in his ability to hold together the fragile center of our conflicted lives. Honesty about our complicity in evil yields a sense of humility as its corollary. Accepting that our lives are problematic urges caution when we judge the truth claims of others. Niebuhr has the self-reflexive habit of living within the truth of his teaching, chuckling at his own pretension as an expert on human imperfections. In the end, truthful self-recognition is the supreme value that provides joy and a sense of liberation. In 1933, he wrote that "the world is in moral confusion partly because religion is not fulfilling its task of helping people to know themselves."[19] This is not the same as the garden-variety versions of happiness that preach to us about living well and accomplishing much.

For Niebuhr, the popular view of happiness assumes we are securely in charge, not merely of our moral choices, but of their complex outcomes. He observes:

> There are no simple congruities in life or history. The cult of happiness erroneously assumes them. It is possible to soften the incongruities of life endlessly by the scientific conquest of nature's caprices, and the social and political triumph over historic injustice. But all such strategies cannot finally overcome the fragmentary character of human existence. The final wisdom of life requires, not the annulment of incongruity but the achievement of serenity within and above it.[20]

As we've seen, a steady state is not on offer in our daily existence. Characteristically, in a sermon called "The Peace of God," the final chapter in *Discerning the Signs of the Times,* Niebuhr speaks about a sense of being forgiven as the "peace of God that passes understanding." The final aim of life arises not through docile tranquility or through self-effort but amid deep awareness that the moral conflicts of conscience have been assuaged.

In addition to this sense of being forgiven, our ability to forgive others points to the self-transcending dimension of our lives. In our better moments this capacity enables us to laugh at our foibles. Niebuhr cited the humorist Will Rogers the way some of us cite Garrison Keillor as wiser (and certainly less pompous) on the human condition than many big-name preachers, theologians, or political pundits. I've noted that the *New York Times* reported on Niebuhr's first sermon after the thirty-six-year-old arrived in Manhattan from Detroit.[21] It tells us a great deal about Niebuhr that a *Times* reporter was dispatched to hear so youthful a preacher. Niebuhr knew that humorists traffic in life's daily struggles, incongruities, and contradictions. Today the social-political satire of Comedy Central's *Daily Show* and *The Colbert Report* performs a similar function. Humor and self-irony keep us honest, point to our common human foibles, and help us live with shattered hopes and deferred dreams about our future and that of our children. The one-time *Saturday Review* editor and writer Norman Cousins taught us from his own life with disease that laughter is healing.[22] Sometimes it's the only way to keep from crying.

Admittedly, when Niebuhr talks about humor and faith, there is little that is lighthearted. In a sermon on humor, he reminds us that God only laughs once in the Bible, in Psalm 2:2. It is not idle laughter but the laughter of scorn directed toward his wayward people: "He that sitteth in the heavens shall laugh. He shall have them in derision." The point might be passed over, except for the fact that Niebuhr's theological naysayers think that he has sold out to culture and has no appreciation of divine judgment. In his usage, the metaphors and anthropomorphic language attributed to God imply a real relationship with the ground of the universe, the mysterious source of right and wrong.

Kierkegaard writes tellingly about a need to distinguish between irony and humor. So does Niebuhr. Irony traffics more deeply in our inwardness, the dimensions of selfhood that we find hard to express and share with neighbors and friends. Humor may simply consist of recognizing incongruity in others, as in the proverbial pratfall of a pompous politician. Irony is subtler; to the rational mind it seems like lying. We say one thing but we mean another. Irony pays tribute to an audience when they "get it" and discern its underlying meaning.[23] The same activity points to the self-transcendence of a writer or speaker, who holds back and reveals at the same time. To the literary-poetic mind, irony is a way of recognizing that deeper, hidden truths must sometimes remain concealed. To share them directly may expose them to ridicule or to hurtful rejoinder.

The injunction to self-knowledge, a main feature of Western philosophy since Socrates, is deeply present in Niebuhr's work. It was picked up especially by the *Confessions* of St. Augustine, which embraces the Pauline understanding of the human self later taken up by Luther and Kierkegaard. In this way of thinking, repentance, a profound sense of sorrow over one's misdeeds (and sin), lies at the heart of the tradition. In Christian theology, repentance, as a change of heart, can be seen as the last individual self-activity prior to the new life of grace. There is here, then, a degree of Christian Socratism at work, even if Niebuhr, always wary of the philosophical tradition, doesn't speak about his thought this way. Yet I'm convinced that Niebuhr teaches a version of the truth put forth by Socrates: The examined Christian life, should we choose to live it, is not an easy life. Conversely, the unexamined Christian life would be an utter contradiction.

This stance is not easy, even for those who are attracted to Niebuhr. Galen Guengerich, Senior Minister of All Souls Unitarian in New York City, doubtless speaks for many when he writes: "Niebuhr is hard medicine, but necessary. We need to acknowledge the moral hazard of our power as a nation," and then continues, "For me, however, Niebuhr ultimately pays too little attention to the profound longing that lies at the core of the American character—the yearning to embody our ideals."[24] *New York Times* columnist David Brooks, writing in the *Atlantic* in 2002 and speaking at a forum in 2009 shows similar misgivings, as if pessimism about the self were the theologian's final word.[25] Brooks appears to think that Niebuhr is right about sin, but wrong about America. He believes Niebuhr is out of touch with America's natural idealism. Yet negativity accounts for only half of Niebuhr's story. In an age of wishful thinking the bracing realism of his thought better positions and enables our hopes to find realization.

For the Nazi refugee and psychologist Erich Fromm, Niebuhr was obsessive regarding the topic of sin. The son of a rabbi, Fromm drew sustenance on a different point from a New Testament verse that lies behind Marx and Freud, his heroes as the two great masters of modern suspicion: "You shall know the truth and the truth shall set you free" (John 8:32).[26] The verse also fits what I have been saying about Niebuhr and self-knowledge. In his self-reflexive thought, the finger that points at the world situation also points directly at oneself.

Theology, Science, and Modernity

Some secular minds, among them Arthur Schlesinger, Jr., have found Niebuhr's faith unfathomable, even as they laud his prescriptions for humanity. Other secular advocates of political realism doubtless care little or nothing about what Niebuhr has to say theologically or how he is regarded among Christians. We can, however, be sure that advocates of his political realism in the era of the Iraq war are hardly drawn to him, as an "apologist of power,"[27] as if his agenda were to give religious sanction to government policies. Niebuhr never wanted to accede to his brother H. Richard Niebuhr's suspicion that his stance tended to make "Christian love an ambulance driver in the wars of interested and clashing parties."[28] Christian ethics, for Niebuhr, is not confined to pockets of the faithful, but reaches into the corridors of power. An irony in this debate, which would not be lost on Niebuhr, is how much his critics try to occupy his role as critics of culture who draw from the Christian tradition.

In an autobiographical statement from 1956 Niebuhr writes that he does not claim to be a theologian, adding that in addition to teaching Christian social ethics, he dealt in the field of "apologetics."

> I cannot and do not claim to be a theologian. I have taught Christian Social Ethics for a quarter of a century and have also dealt in the ancillary field of 'apologetics.' My avocational interest as a kind of circuit rider in the colleges and universities has prompted an interest in the defense and justification of the Christian faith in a secular age, particularly among what Schleiermacher called Christianity's 'intellectual despisers.' I have never been very competent in the nice points of pure theology; and I must confess that I have not been sufficiently interested heretofore to acquire the competence.[29]

The statement deserves a comment, since we will surely continue to think of Niebuhr as a theologian. The self-description as a Christian apologist (apologia means defense) accurately describes his career. In the passage at hand Niebuhr alludes to the work of his nineteenth-century German theological forebear, Friedrich Schleiermacher, who wrote a famous book in 1799 called *On Religion: Speeches to its Cultured Despisers.*[30] Like his predecessor, Niebuhr has been wrongly taken to be a merely "cultural Christian." Niebuhr's more strident theological critics view the disavowal as a confession of theological incompetence regarding a range of age-old doctrinal expositions. Niebuhr makes no secret of the fact that he has little interest in theological arguments that do not shed light on human existence. In a world defined by the specializations and certitudes of natural and social science, not to mention the noisy claimants to the mantle of Christian orthodoxy, Niebuhr went his own way. His thought is discussed in technical journals of politics or theology; but it did not originate there. For many, if not most, readers that habit of mind is more a virtue than a vice.

By their nature debates between science and religion are probably inconclusive. If I read him rightly, Niebuhr views science and theology, along with Stephen Jay Gould, as having nonoverlapping jurisdictions in their modes of inquiry, though they rest on an unknowable mysterious ground of the universe.[31] Niebuhr was not so much a critic of science as a critic of the excessive confidence exuded by some scientists that their specializations can alter the fundamental conditions of human existence. A passage from "Mystery and Meaning" speaks to the limits of science. "We see through a glass darkly when we seek to understand the world about us; because no natural cause is ever a complete and adequate explanation of the subsequent event."[32] Of course, subsequent events are related to preceding events; the emphasis here is on "complete and adequate." When an oncologist and lab technician are at work, we want as much precision as possible, even if exact prediction within natural processes is limited.

If, in a relative manner, we wish for similar precision in history, that option is not open to us. An agnostic element clings to Niebuhr's account of Christian theology as well as to that of natural science. For Niebuhr our knowledge of the world, like our knowledge of ourselves, remains limited, even when expressed with confidence. Simply put, the complexity of things exceeds our grasp in ways that our fragile selfhood seeks to minimize or deny. He insists that an element of incertitude operates in our grasp of the ways of deity as well as in the ways of scientific explanation. The truth of both is distorted among religious fundamentalists or scientific positivists, even if the descriptive claims of science are more tangible and verifiable than those of theology. For a religious mind like Niebuhr's, it is possible to confess ignorance. In many situations, his faith parallels the faith that Lincoln expressed in his Second Inaugural, namely that "The Almighty has His Own Purposes."[33]

Of course, neurological debates about consciousness and the human brain yield new knowledge in dramatic ways. But however much we humans fit into the cycle of evolution, some features of our makeup stand out. As Niebuhr once put it, the other animals know nothing of *Weltschmerz*. "There is among animals no uneasy conscience and no ambition which tends to transgress all natural bounds and become the source of the highest nobility of spirit and of the most demonic madness."[34] Human anxiety, made so famous in earlier existential philosophy and psychology, cannot be wholly tamed or domesticated. Niebuhr acknowledges the advances made by modern science in the theory of natural causation. "The realm of natural causation is more closed, and less subject to divine intervention, than the biblical world view assumes."[35] But the historical action of humans remains open to indeterminate possibilities of good and evil in ways that confound natural science, just as it does for philosophers, historians, psychotherapists, and theologians.

In all this, Niebuhr's trump card is his ability to explain how, with all the grandeur of human aspiration and consciousness, the world continues to be caught up in levels of depravity (waging of holy wars, genocides, mass starvation of populations, torture, child abuse, sex trafficking) as well as in widespread willingness to pursue self-interested financial utopias at the expense of others, including members of one's own community. It bears repeating that Niebuhr viewed "original sin" as the Christian doctrine that is closest to being empirical. Alongside such realities, we need a daily dose of faith and hope. But an analysis of human nature is also needed that can account for and thereby embolden us to deal wisely with "the children of this world."

A need for this sort of understanding is lacking in much of the currently popular criticism of religion. In *Reason, Faith, and Revolution: Reflections on the God Debate* (2009), Oxford literary critic Terry Eagleton argues that the atheistic voices of Richard Dawkins and Christopher Hitchens embody a naive liberal humanism which refuses to see that "the free flourishing of humanity" is only possible if we are willing to confront the very worst. Eagleton decries the fact that these critics ignore "what Christianity knows as original sin," which he identifies as "the prevalence of greed, idolatry, and delusion, the depth of our instinct to dominate and possess, the dull persistence of injustice and exploitation, the chronic anxiety which leads us to hate, maim, and exploit . . ."[36]

Recent atheistic titles, for all of the publicity that surrounds them, contribute little that is new or permanent to the task of making discriminating judgments about religion. In his romping antireligion diatribe, *God Is Not Great: How Religion Poisons Everything* (2007), Christopher Hitchens condemns liberal religion as well as religious fanaticism, as if religion single-handedly explains all the evil in the world. Hitchens's preface calls for free, unfettered investigations of "philosophy, science, history, and human nature."[37] At the end of his book he writes: "Religion has run out of justifications. Thanks to the telescope and the microscope it no longer offers an explanation of anything important."[38] Despite its large claims, the author's faith in science and liberal rationalism makes no serious contribution to the analysis of human nature or to aspects of religious self-criticism, such as we see in Niebuhr. The book asks us to believe that scientifically educated persons will simply run the world better if they can (somehow) get the public square well rid of religion. After 265 pages, a seven-page conclusion on "The Need for a New Enlightenment," calls for new scientific inquiry, democratized via cyberspace, to banish religions from the discourse. It's a mercifully brief ending to a largely self-satisfied book.

In fact, the ripples and good effects of the original Enlightenment remain at work in the world. Their effect on thinking about religion is well documented and analyzed. Niebuhr dislikes the Enlightenment idea of human perfectibility, but he shares the movement's critical posture. Ever since the eighteenth century, intellectual and moral criticisms of religion have been hallmarks of modernity, closely followed by criticism of the power and privilege of religious institutions within liberal societies. The intellectual critique asks whether, in an age of science, it makes sense to cling to faith in God, while the moral critique raises questions about the potentially destructive fanaticism of true believers. The institutional critique of organized religion arises when we ask how the power and deeds of churches, synagogues, mosques, temples, and monastic traditions relate to the larger culture, and develop a view on whether this is beneficial or not. In all these matters, a reflective, self-critical faith is required; certainty in such matters is not on offer. For Niebuhr, divine proofs are as inconclusive as divine disproofs; the incompleteness of scientific explanation on the truly large questions leaves room for deity. In the end, the moral critique of religion is itself taken up within a reflective religious faith, which is also the repository of our deeply felt moral values.

I've suggested repeatedly that Niebuhr writes, and also thinks, with epistemological modesty. There are limits to what we can truly know—about ourselves, about the world, and certainly about God. He holds that Christianity does not have a corner on worldly wisdom. Just as there is not a Christian Chemistry, there is no exact blueprint for a Christian politics or a Christian society. His habit of mind sorts through the wisdom of the world and borrows appropriately, while placing "the wisdom of the world" in a larger perspective. Writing in his *Institutes of the Christian Religion,* John Calvin also endorses the arts and sciences. As he succinctly puts it: "In despising the gifts we insult the Giver."[39] Terry Eagleton captures this splendidly when he writes:

> The difference between science and theology, as I understand it, is one over whether you see the world as a gift or not; and you cannot resolve this just by inspecting the thing, any more than you can deduce from examining a porcelain vase that it is a wedding present.[40]

For Niebuhr, the vast universe is perceived as a gift. Our moral aims and intellectual beliefs stand beneath a higher, transcendent order of good, whether understood as a "God-given part of the mystery of the universe" or simply named as "the good." We can no more invent a sense of the good than we can invent a proper sense of deity. Without this radically transcendent sense of good, viewed through secular eyes or a deep faith, politics remains a messy form of tribal or national religion. Niebuhr is not a metaphysician. Like most of us, he knows in his heart that we affirm and appeal to a moral order just to get on with our individual and collective lives.

Doubt, Toleration, and True Belief

The most disarming aspect of Niebuhr may well be the discovery of his suspicion of ideology, whether religious or political in nature. He deeply distrusts certitude, especially in the form of smugness. Long before the current U.S. interest in being postpartisan, Niebuhr eyed extreme views with suspicion. His thought teaches us to be wary of "true believers," persons who have never doubted. That seems to go against what we expect from a religious writer. But for Niebuhr an element of moral doubt properly belongs to our self-awareness. That attitude, which has tolerance as its corollary, is principled more than opportunistic. Marilynne Robinson writes that "history up to the present moment tells us again and again that a narrow understanding of faith very readily turns to bitterness and coerciveness. There is something about certitude that makes Christianity un-Christian."[41]

As I read her words Robinson is testifying to the whiff of righteousness that accompanies people who have no moral self-doubt. Niebuhr's view sharply contrasts with the dogmatism we see among political and religious fundamentalists or among the cultivated despisers of religion (writers, intellectuals, natural or social scientists) who think that we can successfully resolve our political affairs if we can (somehow) just rid the world of belief in God. Writing on "Tolerance" for *Collier's Encyclopedia,* Niebuhr states:

> The fact is that any commitment, religious political or cultural, can lead to intolerance if there is not a residual awareness of the possibility of error in the truth in which we believe, and of the possibility of truth in the error against which we contend. It is an ironic fact that the modern generation which celebrated its emancipation from traditional religious fanaticisms has been engulfed in the strife between fanatic political creeds which did not allow any community at all except on the basis of political conformity.[42]

For Niebuhr, knowing that we lack full certitude on our most important choices leads to greater mental exertion and realistic hope, not to cynicism and despair. On balance his stance helps us make sober choices and accept limits in ourselves and in using the earth's resources. Even if we must continually seek to ward off fanatical religion, it is wide of the mark to proclaim, in the words of Christopher Hitchens's best seller, that "religion poisons everything."

Despite my best efforts Niebuhr still remains elusive, hard to sum up. NPR (*Speaking of Faith*) host Krista Tippett posed the most difficult question of all when she recently asked whether there's a place for Niebuhr's complexity in the lives of busy Americans. On this, I share the response of her interlocutor, political philosopher Jean Bethke Elshtain, that "we're in very big trouble, if there isn't."[43] If we apply a long view of history to Niebuhr, we can be sure that we have not heard the last word about him. The odd fact is that the trumpeter of human sinfulness appeals to our better selves. Like St. Paul in the New Testament, Niebuhr has a constant vision of the good before his eyes. Of course, his tough-minded resolve doesn't square with standard versions of American optimism. But if his analysis of the human self is true, we should expect the impulsive naturalism of our condition to resist recognizing this fact. Acts of authentic self-recognition are painful and difficult to bear.

In writing this book I have tried to avoid playing "what would Niebuhr say" with respect to subsequent history. That said, the conventional view holds that Niebuhr would have sanctioned the 2001 invasion of Afghanistan as necessary to square off against al-Qaeda, though not the larger invasion of Iraq in 2003, where it wasn't in the least clear that the United States was under attack, and the idea of invading on humanitarian grounds may have seemed just, but only at the expense of public order. Of course, we do not know in detail what Niebuhr would have written or said about the Iraq war, either before or after the 2008 surge. We only know that he would not have been silent on the arrogant use of American power. The contingency of historical events and the unfinished nature of the Iraq war as it relates to overall U.S. policy in the Middle East urge caution. Ethicist Edmund Santurri warns that "it's difficult to judge what Niebuhr might have said about the Iraq war *in toto*."[44]

As I finish working on this book a great Niebuhr buzz has arisen in connection with Barack Obama's Nobel Peace Prize acceptance address, given in Oslo, December 10, 2009. That remarkable speech establishes a high point in the president's self-avowed Niebuhrianism, a theme that runs through the pages of this book. I agree with a spate of editorials that identify the profoundly Niebuhrian contours of the Oslo Peace Prize address: the sense that war is sometimes needed to confront evil, but that this must always be a measured undertaking, entered with a sense of human tragedy and not as a holy crusade.[45] Historians of U.S. foreign policy will pour over the address and assess it further in light of subsequent events. For the moment, I am sure of only one thing: Barack Obama's eloquent espousal of Niebuhrian political theory does not ensure that the president's specific judgments and decisions—apparently based on that theory—would receive Niebuhr's approbation. It's difficult to say how Niebuhr would view ongoing U.S. military engagements in Afghanistan, Pakistan, and other parts of the world. But we can be assured that he would assess these situations with a critical eye. The complexity of Niebuhr's moral imagination, his keen sense of the folly of attempting to manage history, and his profound concern for innocent human life should give us pause.

The fact that political figures and pundits invoke Niebuhr does not mean that his reflection on politics, religion, and Christian faith speaks to or resolves all of today's pressing issues. Confusion reigns supreme if we casually apply the epithets "liberal" or "conservative" to his views. Theological catchwords applied to his teaching (neoorthodox, Christian realist, prophetic) sometimes help, but always need to be explained. Too much reliance on labels skews the central issues of his tragic yet hopeful vision. Broadly speaking, Niebuhr belongs "within the extended family of liberalisms" in theology and in politics.[46] His use of critical reason and historical criticism marks the liberalism of his religious thought. Aware that the word "liberalism" has contradictory political definitions (freedom of restraints in economic life versus establishing minimal standards of human welfare), Niebuhr champions the latter and calls for a "realistic liberalism."[47] Such a realism must rescue the "aristocratic-conservative tradition" from its pretension and "incorporate it into the wisdom by which the life of the community must be regulated and integrated."[48] Although a socialist and pacifist in his early years, he shifted his views for the bulk of his career, largely through study of the social and economic impact of the New Deal. He favored a mixed economy and free market, while seeking to minimize illusions about its beneficence. He thought that people and governments must incessantly work for the common good and criticized the ideology of the free market economy when practiced without checks and balances. But he never did so in a doctrinaire manner.

Advocates of what Arthur Schlesinger, Jr., called the "vital center"[49] in American politics need to see that for Niebuhr as theologian "vital center" refers to the political middle ground as it relates to the mystery of the self, the way that we seek to live with integrity amid the contradictions of our existence. The history and prospects for "Christian realism" are well analyzed alongside contemporary political-social theories in the most recent work of Robin W. Lovin.[50] Like the late Langdon Gilkey, Lovin grasps how Niebuhr's Christian realism "neatly reverses the understanding of the relationship between personal and political ethics that prevails in most of the Christian tradition." Lovin continues:

> Instead of finding a Christian understanding of the moral life most completely expressed in personal relationships and intimate communities where self-giving love often prevails over fear, pride and selfishness, Christian realism proposes that the range of moral possibilities and problems with which we have to deal becomes clear in the political relationships where we pursue happiness, seek security, and construct systems of justice. . . .[51]

The status of the adjective "Christian" in this epithet deserves a comment. Niebuhrian realism must be understood in *his* Christian sense, not in *that of others.* Increasingly in the American media the term "Christian" connotes a narrowly restricted evangelical faith, often leaning to the right or the far right politically. It's a trend that faltering mainline and liberal churches know all too well as they invent strategies to get attention. Hence the Christian elements of Niebuhr are a hard sell for many thoughtful people. Either they are suspicious of him as an idiosyncratic or heterodox, if not a heretical, thinker, or they find any allusions to Christian symbols and teaching an unneeded distraction from the urgent demands of our moral and political existence.

Throughout his work, Niebuhr is a master of suspicion. But he performs these functions to move us to postures of hope and realistic action. The world situation faced by a newly elected President Obama makes this book especially timely. Our concerns with realism in American foreign policy, the breakdown of the global financial system, the rise of religious fanaticisms that feed ideologies of terror, and the global environmental crisis were all addressed by Niebuhr. *Reflections on the End of an Era* (1932) castigated the "mechanism" of a supposedly benevolent market system, which "makes human life seem to be a series of highly rational social relationships and hides the fact that these relations are actually the product, not of mind and conscience but of power and impulse."[52] To the end of his life, Niebuhr drew the lessons of life in conflict with itself and related this insight to the social and moral teachings of religion. Niebuhr's ideas, shaped so much by Christian theology and Judaism, bear on the human situation as construed within Islamic, Buddhist, and Hindu traditions, as well as other forms of modern quasi religion, including the religion of nationalism, and their secular, humanistic alternatives. The economic, political, and religious quandaries we face today were hardly unknown in the era when his thought first took shape.

Contrary to stereotypes, even strong religious belief offers no panacea for coping with life's dilemmas. Major Christian writers and those of other traditions know that an acknowledgment of suffering and the rocky road of human existence lies at the heart of authentic religion. The life of faith is elusive and the tasks of life are hard. The way we face moral conflict holds believers and nonbelievers together in a common humanity. The most serious Christian writers appear to know these things. Thus Kierkegaard's pseudonym for *Fear and Trembling,* Johannes de Silentio, tells us that

> faith is the highest passion in a human being. . . . But life has tasks enough, even for one who fails to come as far as faith, and when he loves these honestly life won't be a waste either, even if it can never compare with that of those who had a sense of the highest and grasped it.[53]

To wrestle long and hard with clashes between rival loyalties and moral imperatives (home, family, work, nation, global humanity, and the earth) is itself worthy of high honor. The message is this: We can all respect the common struggles of humanity, even if we stop short of a fully formed life of faith.

Reinhold Niebuhr holds that politics and theology, unlike science and theology, do have overlapping jurisdictions. Both bring a body of theory to bear on the practices of human communities. Both focus on humanity, its aspirations, and its fate. Of course, proper theology begins and ends with a sense of deity, something not necessarily required for politics. That said, politics and theology can be distinguished more readily than separated. Both grow out of a complex view of human nature, interpreted through our religious, philosophical, and political traditions. It's a mistake to think that the Christian dimension of Niebuhr could ever be separated from his politics.

In her 1957 memoir, *Memories of a Catholic Girlhood,* novelist Mary McCarthy wrote that "religion is only good for good people." In putting matters this way McCarthy was personally reacting to the narrow-minded cruelty enacted in the name of God during her strict Catholic schooling and upbringing. Holding that religion is only good for good people seems to fly in the face of anyone who believes in sin and a need for forgiveness. Her idea plants a moral marker as baseline for judging the truth of religion. It's a way of viewing "the gods" that is as old as Plato's *Euthyphro.* Is an act moral because the gods do it, or do the gods do it because it is moral? In the eighteenth-century Enlightenment Kant and Lessing also subjected religious dogma and practice to a moral test. If Niebuhr does the same, it's done for a different reason, one that he shares with Judaism. Rightly understood, both religions—today we would want to add Islam as well—view morality as the heart of religion.

In taking up McCarthy's idea in his 1960 farewell address to students at Union Theological Seminary Niebuhr gave her utterance his own twist, saying that religion is "only good for people with inner honesty." He thereby signaled that a sense of the good must be applied self-critically to one's own deeds. We've come full circle to the conflicted self of St. Paul, "The good that I would I cannot do" of Romans, chapter 7. The farewell address warns against the rise of a morally vacuous religious obscurantism among Protestants. Niebuhr teaches that none of us is well-served by denying modernity, the life of the mind, and historical criticism not just of religion but of all the other belief systems and ideas that seek to supplant the classical faiths. His warning pertains to today as much as it did when first spoken.

Religion for Niebuhr is not primarily otherworldly. Yet the theological dimension of Niebuhr's earth-bound politics deserves our attention. The faith of the Psalmist, so much a part of Niebuhr's outlook, is similarly earthbound. "Do not fret because of the wicked; do not be envious of wrongdoers, for they will soon fade like the grass, and wither like the green herb" (Ps. 37: 1–2). A religion of rewards and punishments in the hereafter is not within the Psalmist's purview. Instead, the consequences of our moral choices play out in the world as we live in it, and well beyond that point. We live near the edge of a slippery slope where envy and pride lead to our downfall. Niebuhr's religious faith was not a separate realm that he kept on hand for use in seminary teaching or when sermonizing around the country. Like his brother, H. Richard, Reinhold Niebuhr stood close to Judaism all his life. Toward the end of his life he developed a great friendship with his Morningside Heights neighbor, the Jewish theologian Abraham Heschel. Like a believing Jew, Niebuhr saw himself living "between the times" in a situation where the traditional Jewish longing for a Messiah is replaced by the hope of a Second Coming.

In fact, Niebuhr's theology is almost as steeped in the Hebrew Bible (Old Testament) as it is in St. Paul and the Gospels. Far from that making him heretical, he sees the New Testament as fundamentally carrying forth the same intrinsic message. If Niebuhr breaks with a form of traditional Christian teaching, it is supersessionism—the view held for two thousand years that Christian truth supplants that of Judaism.[54] Christians, Niebuhr holds, have no business trying to convert Jews in order to bring them to the God that they already know.

As a Christian, Niebuhr shares with the Hebrew prophets the view that religious faith, morality, and politics are tightly interwoven.[55] Although our moral will is easily distorted and our knowledge limited, the fate of the earth is still up to us. Faith and politics are not identical; yet, in both cases, having a sense of epistemological modesty and openness to surprise helps keep us sane. The theistic perspective claims a universality that is greater than a nation-state or the collective relations between nations. The transcendent dimension of religion, the fact that for Niebuhr it includes the mystery of God, exceeds the bounds that we associate with political thought. Thinking about religion is more all-encompassing and less empirical than politics. Yet the aims of politics, like those of religion, are often elusive; the tasks we are called to undertake remain incomplete in the span of our lives. That's essentially the message of this book. In the last analysis, Niebuhr the political philosopher and Niebuhr the Christian thinker are one and the same. A theological view of the world animates and unites his political and religious thought. His dual-edged faith accords with the ancient commandment of Micah 6:8 "to do justice, and to love kindness, and to walk humbly with your God."

NOTES

CHAPTER 1

1. Reinhold Niebuhr, *Reflections on the End of an Era* (New York: Charles Scribner's Sons, 1934), ix.

2. *C&C* became the virtual house organ for disseminating the views of Niebuhr and his close associates. Mark Hulsether, *Building a Protestant Left: Christianity and Crisis Magazine 1941–1993* (Knoxville, TN: University of Tennessee Press, 1999).

3. Isaiah Berlin, *The Hedgehog and the Fox: An Essay on Tolstoy's View of History* (London: Weidenfeld & Nicolson, 1953), 10.

4. Martin E. Marty, "Reinhold Niebuhr: Public Theology and the American Experience," *Journal of Religion* 54 (1974): 332–359, serves as a benchmark for Niebuhr interpretation in the 1970s.

5. Arthur Schlesinger, Jr., "Reinhold Niebuhr's Long Shadow," *New York Times*, June 22, 1992, and "Forgetting Reinhold Niebuhr," *New York Times*, September 18, 2005.

6. Richard Wightman Fox, *Reinhold Niebuhr: A Biography* (New York: Pantheon Books, 1985); reviewed by Roger Shinn, "Reinhold Niebuhr: A Reverberating Voice," *Christian Century* (January 1–8, 1986).

7. Robert McAfee Brown, "Reinhold Niebuhr: His Theology in the 1980s," and Michael Novak, "Reinhold Niebuhr: Model for Neoconservatives," *Christian Century* (January 22, 1986), 66–68, and 69–71; Robert McAfee Brown, ed., *The Essential Reinhold Niebuhr: Selected Essays and Addresses* (New Haven,

CT: Yale University Press, 1986) remains a splendid collection of representative Niebuhr texts.

8. Ronald H. Stone, *Professor Reinhold Niebuhr: A Mentor to the Twentieth Century* (Louisville, KY: Westminster/John Knox Press, 1992), Charles C. Brown, *Niebuhr and His Age: Reinhold Niebuhr's Prophetic Role and Legacy* (Harrisburg, PA: Trinity Press International, 1992).

9. Charles C. Brown, *Niebuhr and His Age;* Henry B. Clark, *Serenity, Courage and Wisdom: The Enduring Legacy of Reinhold Niebuhr* (Cleveland, OH: Pilgrim Press, 1994); Gabriel Fackre, *The Promise of Reinhold Niebuhr*, rev. ed. (Lanham, MD: University Press of America, 1994); and Robin W. Lovin, *Reinhold Niebuhr and Christian Realism* (Cambridge: Cambridge University Press, 1995).

10. Larry Rasmussen, ed., *Reinhold Niebuhr: Theologian of Public Life* (Minneapolis, MN: Fortress Press, 1991), "Introduction," 1–41; Edmund N. Santurri, *Perplexity in the Moral Life: Philosophical and Theological Considerations* (Charlottesville, VA: University Press of Virginia, 1987), especially 165–181, and "Global Justice after the Fall: Christian Realism and the 'Law of Peoples,'" *Journal of Religious Ethics* 33.4 (December 2005), 783–814 plus 34.3, 523–530, For David Little's comment and Santurri's response; Langdon Gilkey, *On Niebuhr: A Theological Study* (Chicago, IL: University of Chicago Press, 2001); Robin W. Lovin, *Christian Realism and the New Realities* (Cambridge: Cambridge University Press, 2008).

11. Robert D. Kaplan, *The Coming Anarchy: Shattering the Dreams of the Post Cold War* (New York: Vintage Books, 2000), 65, who quotes a passage from *The Irony of American History* (1952), 74.

12. Robert D. Kaplan, "Looking the World in the Eye," *Atlantic* (December 2001), reports Huntington saying, "I am a child of Niebuhr," in accounting for his moral vision and practical realism.

13. Don Richardson, ed., *Conversations with Carter* (Boulder, CO: Lynne Rienner Publishers, 1998), 13, 39.

14. Larry Rasmussen, "Reinhold Niebuhr: Public Theologian," *Cross Currents* 28 (Summer 1988): 198, citing Robert Marguand, "In Search of 'Public Intellectuals,"*Christian Science Monitor*, December 14, 1987, 19.

15. Gary Dorrien, *Imperial Designs: Neoconservatism and the New Pax Americana* (New York: Routledge, 2004); Niall Ferguson, *Colossus: the Price of America's Empire* (New York: Penguin Press, 2004); Michael Ignatieff, "The American Empire: The Burden" *New York Times Magazine* (January 5, 2003); Chalmers Johnson, *Nemesis: The Last Days of the American Republic* (New York: Henry Holt and Company, 2006); Clyde V. Prestowitz, *Rogue Nation: American Unilateralism and the Failure of Good Intentions* (New York: Basic Books, 2003); Cornel West, *Democracy Matters: Winning the Fight Against Imperialism* (New York: Penguin Press, 2004).

16. Reinhold Niebuhr, *The Irony of American History*, with a new introduction by Andrew J. Bacevich (Chicago, IL and London: University of Chicago Press, 2008), ix. See also Bacevich, *American Empire: The Realities and Consequences of U.S. Diplomacy* (2004), *The New American Militarism: How Americans are Seduced by War* (New York: Oxford University Press, 2005), "Prophets and Poseurs: Niebuhr and Our Times," *World Affairs: A Journal of Ideas and Debate* (Winter 2008), and *The Limits of Power: The End of American Exceptionalism* (New York: Henry Holt and Company, 2008).

17. David Brooks's *New York Times* column, April 26, 2007, mentioned *The Irony of American History* in the context of his interview with Barack Obama.

18. Carl M. Cannon, "Untruth and Consequences," *Atlantic* (January/February 2007).

19. James Fallows, national correspondent for the *Atlantic*, comments on the timeliness of Niebuhr's piece "Awkward Imperialist" from May 1930 (July/August 2006); *Washington Post* columnist E. J. Dionne, Jr. *Souled Out: Reclaiming Faith and Politics after the Religious Right* (Princeton University Press, 2008); former *New Republic* editor, Peter Beinart, *The Good Fight: Why Liberals—and Only Liberals—Can Win the War on Terror and Make America Great Again* (New York: HarperCollins, 2006); historian Kevin Mattson, *When America Was Great: The Fighting Faith of Postwar Liberalism* (New York / London: Routledge, 2004); *New York Times* columnist David Brooks touched on Niebuhr some ten times between May 2004 and August 2008 (*NYT* Archive); Pepperdine University writer Joseph Loconte, "The War Party's Theologian," *Wall Street Journal*, May 31, 2002 and "The Irony of American Politics," *Books and Culture: A Christian Review* (November/December 2008), 29–30, which reviews *The Irony of American History* (2008).

20. Anatol Lieven and John Hulsman, *Ethical Realism: A Vision for America's Role in the World* (New York: Pantheon Books, 2006).

21. *Speaking of Faith* Web page, "Moral Man and Immoral Society: The Public Theology of Reinhold Niebuhr," http://speakingoffaith.publicradio.org/programs/niebuhr-rediscovered.

22. Senator John Danforth, *Faith and Politics: How the "Moral Values" Debate Divides America and How to Move Forward Together* (New York: Viking, 2006), 37.

23. Bill Moyers's PBS shows discussing Niebuhr featured James Cone (November 23, 2007), http://www.pbs.gen.in/moyers/journal/11232007/transcript3.html and Andrew J. Bacevich (August 15, 2008), http://www.pbs.org/moyers/journal/08152008/profile.html.

24. David Brooks put it this way during an NPR *Speaking of Faith* forum on "The Legacy of Reinhold Niebuhr and the Future of Christian Realism" at

the Berkley Center for Religion, Peace, and World Affairs, Georgetown University, January 29, 2009.

25. David Brooks, "Obama, Gospel and Verse," *New York Times*, April 26, 2007.

26. Michael Gerson, "The Irony of Obama," *Real Clear Politics*, Web site (October 22, 2008).

27. Michiko Kakutani, "From Books, New President Found Voice," *New York Times*, January 19, 2009, lists "works of Reinhold Niebuhr" without specifying titles.

28. Including, among others, Marilynne Robinson, Toni Morrison, Ralph Waldo Emerson, the Bible, Shakespeare's histories and tragedies.

29. Cited in Rasmussen, "Introduction," *Reinhold Niebuhr*, 15–16.

30. Isaiah Berlin, *The Crooked Timber of Humanity: Chapters in the History of Ideas*, ed. Henry Hardy (Princeton, NJ: Princeton University Press, 1990), citing the idea from Kant's *Idea for a Universal History from a Cosmopolitan Point of View* (1784).

31. The *Time* piece was written by then senior editor Whittakar Chambers, ex-Communist and spy-informant famous for his role in the Alger Hiss trial and a careful student of Niebuhr's thought.

32. Niebuhr Papers, LC, Box 17.

33. Of course, none of the figures cited worked as an academic theologian.

34. That *Nature and Destiny* was never translated into German has been confirmed by library searches as well as through communication with Professor Dietz Lange of Göttingen, Germany, whose PhD dissertation on Niebuhr was written in the early 1960s. A translation was in process of being negotiated in 1946; see the letter to Ursula Niebuhr from Stuttgart, September 8, 1946, in *Remembering Reinhold Niebuhr*, 202.

35. Arthur Schlesinger, Jr., "Forgetting Reinhold Niebuhr," *New York Times*, September 18, 2005.

CHAPTER 2

1. For years considered passé, Toynbee's work is again being recognized in the era of globalization. See Parag Khanna, *The Second World: How Emerging Powers Are Redefining Global Competition in the Twenty-first Century* (New York: Random House, 2009).

2. James Fallows, writing on the occasion of the magazine's 150th anniversary, *Atlantic*, (July/August 2006).

3. Reinhold Niebuhr, *Beyond Tragedy: Essays on the Christian Interpretation of History* (New York: Charles Scribner's Sons, 1937), 29, hereafter cited as *BT*.

4. H. Richard Niebuhr, *The Meaning of Revelation* (New York: Macmillan, 1941), 48.

5. David Bromwich, "Self-Deceptions of Empire," *London Review of Books* (October 23, 2008), 12–13, review of *The Irony of American History*.

6. A cardinal sin of work in the humanities is "essentialism," acting as if there is a common core that holds together cultural entities. On this view, there is no Christianity, only diverse and contradictory subgroups that use this name. A widely read book by Wilfred Cantwell Smith, *The Meaning and End of Religion* (1964) contended similarly that there is no such thing as "religion."

7. Niebuhr Papers, LC, Box 10. Schlesinger comments that the book is "wise, valuable, and illuminating."

8. Arthur M. Schlesinger, Jr., *The Age of Roosevelt: Crisis of the Old Order 1919–1933* (Boston, MA: Houghton Mifflin, 2003), originally published in 1957.

9. *New York Times*, "Folly's Antidote," January 1, 2007.

10. *The Prophets* (New York: Harper and Row, 1962), 23.

11. *The Prophets*, 21.

12. Cicero, *Orator* xxxiv, 120, tr. H. M. Hubbell (London: William Heinemann, 1962), 395, more literally: "To be ignorant of what occurred before you were born is to remain always a child."

13. G. W. F. Hegel, *Reason in History*, tr. Robert S. Hartman (Indianapolis, IN: Bobbs-Merrill, 1953), 8.

14. *The Nature and Destiny of Man* I (New York: Charles Scribner's Sons, 1941), 1, hereafter cited as *NDM* I or *NDM* II. Niebuhr consistently uses the term "man" in the archaic sense to mean humanity.

15. Use of the term "self," borrowed from classical German philosophy, allowed Niebuhr to speak of the human without in the same breath sorting out the roles of the biological and mental.

16. *NDM* I, 4.

17. John R. Searle, *The Mystery of Consciousness* (New York: New York Review of Books, 1997), xiii. The book includes exchanges with Daniel C. Dennett and David J. Chalmers.

18. "The Christian Faith and Humanism," Lecture at Union Theological Seminary, 1952, from The Reinhold Niebuhr Audio Collection, Union-PSCE in Richmond, Virginia, CD N665 3–4.

19. The 1967 aphorism captures what Niebuhr had written for the *Atlantic* in 1954 in "History as Drama": "We can learn from historical analogies but we must not rely upon them too much simply because, when 'history repeats itself' it never does so exactly." Niebuhr Papers, LC, Box 16.

20. Plato, *Phaedrus* 266, tr. W. C. Helmbold and W. G. Rabinowitz (Indianapolis, IN: Bobbs-Merrill, 1956), 56.

21. Bacevich, "Introduction," *The Irony of American History*, ix–xx.

22. "Augustine's Political Realism," in *Christian Realism and Political Problems* (New York: Charles Scribner's Sons, 1953), 120.

23. Plato, *Cratylus* 428d, tr. Benjamin Jowett, in *Collected Dialogues*, eds. Edith Hamilton and Huntington Cairns (New York: Pantheon Books, 1961).

24. Nassim Nicholas Taleb, *Fooled by Randomness: The Hidden Role of Chance in Life and in the Markets* (New York: Random House, 2004).

25. David Brooks, *New York Times*, October 28, 2008.

26. Malcolm Gladwell, *Outliers: The Story of Success* (New York: Little, Brown and Company, 2008), 19, adding, "It makes a difference where and when we grew up. The culture we belong to and the legacies passed down by our forebears shape the patterns of our achievement in ways we cannot begin to imagine. It's not enough to ask what successful people are like, in other words. It is only by asking where they are *from* that we can unravel the logic behind who succeeds and who doesn't."

27. *NDM* II, 49.

28. *Faith and History: A Comparison of Christian and Modern Views of History* (New York: Charles Scribner's Sons, 1949), 142.

29. *NDM* II, 3.

30. *Faith and History*, 137.

31. *NDM* II, 52.

32. *NDM* II, 58.

33. *NDM* II, 2.

34. *NDM* II, 109–110, n.6.

35. The argument is given in a section of Kierkegaard's *Philosophical Fragments*, called "Interlude," eds. Howard V. Hong and Edna H. Hong (Princeton, NJ: Princeton University Press, 1985), 72–88.

36. "Philosophy is perfectly right in saying that life must be understood backward. But then one forgets the other clause—that it must be lived forward. The more one thinks through this clause, the more one concludes that life in temporality never becomes properly understandable, simply because never at any time does one get perfect repose to take a stance—backward." *Journals and Papers* (1843), cited in Howard V. Hong and Edna H. Hong, eds., *The Essential Kierkegaard* (Princeton, NJ: Princeton University Press, 2000), 12.

37. Marilynne Robinson, "Credo," *Harvard Divinity Bulletin* (Spring 2008), 26.

38. Marilynne Robinson, *Gilead* (New York: Farrar, Straus and Giroux, 2004), 166.

39. http://www.bestsermons.net/1926/The_Foolishness_of_Preaching.html

40. Cited in the 1960 sermon, "We See Through a Glass Darkly," in Reinhold Niebuhr, *Justice and Mercy*, ed. Ursula M. Niebuhr (San Francisco, CA: Harper & Row, 1974), 33.

CHAPTER 3

1. *Reflections on the End of an Era*, p. ix.

2. See "Augustine's Political Realism," *Christian Realism and Political Problems* (New York: Charles Scribner's Sons, 1953), 119–146.

3. Eric Gregory, *Politics and the Order of Love: An Augustinian Ethic of Democratic Citizenship* (Chicago, IL: University of Chicago Press, 2008), 21, 256.

4. *NDM* I, 59.

5. Søren Kierkegaard, *Two Ages: The Age of Revolution and the Present Age. A Literary Review*, orig. 1846, eds., Howard V. Hong and Edna H. Hong (Princeton, NJ: Princeton University Press, 1978), 100.

6. *Two Ages*, 79.

7. Niebuhr quoted Kierkegaard, *Sickness unto Death: A Christian Psychological Exposition for Edification and Awakening*, tr. Alastair Hannay (New York: Penguin Books, 1989) in German translation in the late 1930s before Kierkegaard had appeared in English. Part I explores the morphology of despair by exploring our ambivalence in wanting to be (or wanting not to be) a certain kind of self.

8. *NDM I*, 228.

9. *The Irony of American History* frequently speaks of our need to act with a sense of responsibility toward the world community.

10. John Dominic Crossan, *The Dark Interval: Towards a Theology of Story* (Sonoma, CA: Polebridge Press, 1988), 99.

11. See Jean Bethke Elshtain, *Augustine and the Limits of Politics* (Notre Dame, IN: University of Notre Dame Press, 1995), especially chapter 3, "Against the Pridefulness of Philosophy."

12. Frank Rich, "The Best Are Not Always the Brightest," *New York Times*, December 7, 2008.

13. *Moral Man and Immoral Society: A Study in Ethics and Politics* (New York: Charles Scribner's Sons, 1932), xi–xii, hereafter cited as *MMIS*. In 1927 he had already written, "There is an increasing tendency among modern men to imagine themselves ethical because they have delegated their vices to larger and larger groups." *Love and Justice: Selections from the Shorter Writings of Reinhold Niebuhr*, ed. D. B. Robertson (Louisville, KY: Westminster/John Knox Press: 1957), 243.

14. Langdon Gilkey, *On Niebuhr: A Theological Study*, 4, records the shocked disbelief of liberal Protestants of his father's generation, including Harry Emerson Fosdick, upon the publication of *Moral Man and Immoral Society*.

15. Reinhold Niebuhr, *Man's Nature and His Communities* (New York: Charles Scribner's Sons, 1965), 22.

16. Niebuhr argued long and hard for a nonvindictive approach to the recovery of Germany and Japan, while the work of the contemporary truth and reconciliation inquiry in South Africa provides a telling example of conscience working at the national level.

17. Ralph Blumenthal, "If Bernie Met Dante," *New York Times*, March 15, 2009, Week in Review, 2, cites poet laureate and Dante scholar Robert Pinsky to the effect that the lowest, ninth circle of hell holds the betrayers of family, country, political faction, and benefactors.

18. *MMIS*, 243. "Gandhi is not less sincere or morally less admirable because considerations of political efficacy partly determine his policies and qualify the purity of the doctrine of 'ahimsa' to which he is committed" (244).

19. *War as Crucifixion. Essays on Peace, Violence and 'Just war,'* the *Christian Century*, eds., John M. Buchanan and David Heim (Chicago, IL, 2002), includes a sharp exchange of views between H. Richard Niebuhr, "The Grace of Doing Nothing," and Reinhold Niebuhr, "Must We Do Nothing?"

20. *An Interpretation of Christian Ethics* (New York: Harper & Brothers, 1935).

21. *An Interpretation of Christian Ethics*, 9–10.

22. *Reinhold Niebuhr: His Religious, Social, and Political Thought*, eds. Charles W. Kegley and Robert W. Bretall (New York: Macmillan, 1956), 434–435.

23. From a sermon on Mt. 5:43–48, given at Union Seminary in 1952, in *The Essential Reinhold Niebuhr*, 33.

24. Aristotle's *Ethics* teaches the same idea of good and evil as immeasurable.

25. More literally: "Are you giving me the evil eye because I am good?"

26. "Love and Law in Protestantism and Catholicism," *The Essential Reinhold Niebuhr*, 153.

27. From "The Christian Church in a Secular Age," an address at the Oxford Life and Work Conference 1937 in *The Essential Reinhold Niebuhr*, 86.

28. David L. Chappell, *A Stone of Hope: Prophetic Religion and the Death of Jim Crow* (Chapel Hill, NC: University of North Carolina Press, 2004), 51

29. Although "forgiveness of sins" occurs in the articles of the Western Apostles Creed, there is no mention of sin in the original Nicene Creed (325) of the Greek tradition.

30. Abraham Heschel, "A Hebrew Evaluation of Reinhold Niebuhr," in *Reinhold Niebuhr*, eds. Kegley and Bretall, 407.

31. For a spirited debate with his wife on the merits of Episcopal worship, see "Sunday Morning Debate," *Christian Century*, (April 22, 1936), reprinted in Reinhold Niebuhr, *Essays in Applied Christianity* (New York: Meridian Books, 1959), 42–48.

32. The most widely used confession in today's Episcopal Book of Common Prayer reads: "Most merciful God, we confess that we have sinned against you in thought, word, and deed, by what we have done, and by what we have left undone. We have not loved you with our whole heart; we have not loved our neighbors as ourselves. We are truly sorry and we humbly repent. For the sake of your Son Jesus Christ, have mercy on us and forgive us; that we may delight in your will, and walk in your ways, to the glory of your Name. Amen." *The Book of Common Prayer* (New York: Oxford University Press, 1990), 360.

33. Erich Fromm, in response to a question from June Bingham, December 26, 1958, Niebuhr Papers, LC, Box 26.

34. M. Scott Peck, *The Road Less Traveled: A New Psychology of Love, Traditional Values, and Spiritual Growth* (New York: Simon and Schuster, 1978), 271–277.

35. Elaine Pagels, *Adam, Eve, and the Serpent* (New York: Random House, 1988), especially chapters 5 and 6, 98–150.

36. Chapter 6 of this book returns to the topic of the Sojourners movement and Niebuhr.

37. John Shelby Spong, *A New Christianity for a New World: Why Traditional Faith is Dying and How a New Faith is Being Born* (San Francisco, CA: HarperSanFrancisco, 2001), 147–170.

38. On the theme of "hopeful realism" see chapter 4, n. 13 on the work of Douglas F. Ottati.

39. *Man's Nature and His Communities*, 23.

40. Marcus J. Borg, *The Heart of Christianity* (San Francisco, CA: HarperSanFrancisco, 2003), 170.

CHAPTER 4

1. The Thomas Mann letter is dated February 20, 1942, but must be from 1943, since Niebuhr's review appeared in the *Nation* (November 28, 1942); Niebuhr Papers, LC, Box 27.

2. *Time* (March 8, 1948), 71.

3. Harold Pinter obituary, *New York Times*, December 26, 2008.

4. On the significance of Luther's German Bible for the work of Johannes Brahms, see Daniel Beller-McKenna, *Brahms and the German Spirit* (Cambridge, MA: Harvard University Press, 2004).

5. *The Irony of American History*, 63. A letter from *New York Times* columnist James Reston to June Bingham, April 14, 1960, reports that this chapter of the book especially impressed him; Niebuhr Papers, LC, Box 27.

6. David Bromwich, "Self-Deceptions of Empire," *London Review of Books* (October 23, 2008), 13, reviewing *The Irony of American History*.

7. Wilhelm and Marion Pauck, *Paul Tillich: His Life and Thought Volume I: Life* (New York: Harper & Row, 1976), 170.

8. Edward Mendelson, *Later Auden* (New York: Farrar, Straus and Giroux, 1999), 173.

9. Jennifer Leader, "'Certain Axioms Rivaling Scriptures': Marianne Moore, Reinhold Niebuhr, and the Ethics of Engagement," *Twentieth Century Literature* 51, no. 3 (Autumn, 2005): 316–340.

10. See Moore's postcard to the Niebuhrs, New Year's Day 1960; Niebuhr Papers, LC, Box 50.

11. Stephen Dunn, "Provisional Conclusions," an interview in *Books and Culture: A Christian Review* (March 8, 2008).

12. G. A. Studdert Kennedy, *After War, Is Faith Possible?* ed. Kerry Walters (Eugene, OR: Cascade Books, 2008).

13. Douglas F. Ottati, *Hopeful Realism: Reclaiming the Poetry of Theology* (Cleveland, OH: Pilgrim Press, 1999).

14. Niebuhr, *Leaves from the Notebook of a Tamed Cynic* (New York: Meridian Books, 1957), 50, hereafter cited as *LNTC*.

15. *LNTC*, 27.

16. *LNTC*, 72

17. Nathaniel Hawthorne, *The House of Seven Gables* (New York: Signet Classics), 42.

18. *LNTC*, 166.

19. *BT*, 3.

20. *BT*, 289.

21. Marilynne Robinson, "Credo," 22.

22. "Preface," *LNTC*, 9.

23. *LNTC*, 201–202.

24. *Christianity and Crisis* (May 28, 1951), reprinted in *Essays in Applied Christianity*, 59.

25. *Justice and Mercy*, 72, 97.

26. Martin Luther, "The German Mass and Order of Service" (1526), *Liturgies of the Western Church*, ed., Bard Thompson (Philadelphia, PA: Fortress Press, 1961), 132.

27. *Justice and Mercy*, 94.

28. Robert D. Kaplan, *Warrior Politics: Why Leadership Demands a Pagan Ethos* (New York: Random House, 2002), xix–xx.

29. *BT*, 156.

30. Recognizing Stoicism as an impressive path to wisdom and courage, Niebuhr's colleague Paul Tillich paid it tribute as "the only real alternative to Christianity in the Western world." Paul Tillich, *The Courage to Be* (New Haven, CT: Yale University Press, 1952), 9.

31. *Markings*, trs. Leif Sjöberg and W.H. Auden, with a foreword by W. H. Auden (New York: Knopf, 1964).

32. John Milbank, "The Poverty of Niebuhrianism," chapter 10 in *The Word Made Strange: Theology, Language, Culture* (Oxford: Blackwell, 1997).

33. Rainer Maria Rilke, *Poems from the Book of Hours*, tr. by Babette Deutsch (New York: New Directions, 1941), 49.

34. See Elisabeth Sifton, *The Serenity Prayer: Faith and Politics in Times of Peace and War* (New York: W. W. Norton & Company, 2003), especially 292–296. Recurrent doubt about whether Niebuhr originally composed the prayer has again been laid to rest; Laurie Goodstein, "Serenity Prayer Stirs Up Doubt: Who Wrote It?" *New York Times*, July 11, 2008 and "Once in Doubt, Credit for Prayer Won't Change," *New York Times*, November 28, 2009. Written for a village church service in Heath, Massachusetts, in 1943, "The Serenity Prayer" was printed for use by army chaplains in World War II and subsequently adopted by Alcoholics Anonymous.

35. Epictetus, *Handbook of Epictetus*, tr. Nicholas White (Indianapolis, IN: The Hackett Publishing Company, 1983), 12.

36. *Discerning the Sign of the Times*, "The Peace of God" (New York: Charles Scribner's Sons, 1946), 181, hereafter cited as *DST*.

37. Bertolt Brecht, Appendix A: "Writing the Truth: Five Difficulties," *Galileo* (New York: Grove Press, 1966), 139.

38. *DST*, in sermon, "The Peace of God," 178–180.

39. Friedrich Schlegel, *Friedrich Schlegel's Lucinde and the Fragments*, ed. Peter Firchow (Minneapolis, MN: University of Minnesota Press, 1971), 143.

CHAPTER 5

1. Brann, "A Way to Philosophy," *Metaphilosophy* 6, nos. 3–4 (July–October 1975): 359.

2. Cushing Strout, *American Quarterly* 5, no. 2 (Summer 1953): 174–175; C. Page Smith, *William and Mary Quarterly*, 417. Reviewing the book in *The Reporter* in 1952 poet Archibald MacLeish held that Niebuhr denied the human dignity that stands behind America's liberal traditions; Niebuhr Papers, LC, Box 17.

3. *IAH*, 36.

4. *IAH*, 143.

5. *IAH*, 113.

6. *New York Times*, April 26, 2007.

7. Andrew J. Bacevich, "Introduction," *The Irony of American History* (Chicago, IL: University of Chicago Press, 2008), ix. Bacevich is especially impressed with Niebuhr's ability to unmask the arrogance and pretension of

U.S. policy. Andrew J. Bacevich, "Illusions of Managing History: The Enduring Relevance of Reinhold Niebuhr," University Lecture, Boston University, October 9, 2007.

8. *IAH*, 26.

9. *IAH*, 89.

10. *IAH*, 138–147 on preventive wars, 147–150 on Kennan.

11. *IAH*, 134.

12. *IAH*, 88.

13. *IAH*, 53.

14. *IAH*, 54.

15. *IAH*, 61.

16. *IAH*, 33.

17. *IAH*, 5.

18. *IAH*, 36.

19. *IAH*, 56.

20. *IAH*, 100.

21. *IAH*, 41.

22. *IAH*, 103–105.

23. *IAH*, 105.

24. *IAH*, 16.

25. *MMIS*, 91.

26. *IAH*, 69.

27. Michael P. Zuckert, *The Natural Rights Republic* (Notre Dame, IN: University of Notre Dame Press, 1996).

28. Louis P. Masur, "The American Character," *Chronicle Review* (January 16, 2009).

29. Godfrey Hodgson, *The Myth of American Exceptionalism* (New Haven, CT: Yale University Press, 2009).

30. Masur, "The American Character."

31. Seymour Martin Lipset, *American Exceptionalism: A Double-Edged Sword* (New York: W. W. Norton & Company, 1996), 26.

32. *IAH*, 61.

33. *IAH*, 23.

34. See titles in chapter 1, n. 19 and n. 20.

35. *IAH*, 133.

36. *IAH*, 83.

37. *IAH*, 149–150.

38. *IAH*, 174.

39. See chapter 2, n. 19.

CHAPTER 6

1. Elisabeth Sifton, *The Serenity Prayer: Faith and Politics in Times of Peace and War* (New York: W. W. Norton & Company, 2003), 316–317.

2. H. Richard Niebuhr, *Christ and Culture* (New York: HarperCollins, 2001) reissued on its fiftieth anniversary (2001) with a new foreword by Martin E. Marty and a preface by James M. Gustafson; see Douglas F. Ottati, "*Christ and Culture:* Still Worth Reading after All These Years," *Journal of the Society of Christian Ethics* 23, no. 1 (2003): 121–132.

3. *Christ and Culture*, 149.

4. Prominent Reformation historical theologian and close friend of Niebuhr, Wilhelm Pauck, criticized Niebuhr's view of Luther's "cultural defeatism" as not based on careful study of modern Luther research. Wilhelm Pauck, *The Heritage of the Reformation*, revised edition (Glencoe, IL: Free Press, 1961), 12–16.

5. Jim Wallis, *The Great Awakening: Reviving Faith and Politics in a Post-Religious Right America* (New York: HarperCollins, 2008), 261 cites Niebuhr once from a Web site to the effect that "the worst evils in the world are not done by evil people, but by good people who don't know they are not doing good."

6. Jim Wallis and Joyce Hollyday, eds. *Cloud of Witnesses* (Maryknoll, NY: Orbis Books, 2005). Jimmy Carter wrote a foreword to *The Great Awakening* (2008).

7. Jim Wallis, *The Call to Conversion* (New York: HarperCollins, 1981, revised and updated 2005), 78.

8. Jim Wallis expresses his debt to Walter Rauschenbusch, in "What to Do," *Christianity and the Social Crisis of the 21st Century*, ed., Paul B. Rauschenbusch (New York: HarperCollins, 2007), 341–346.

9. *With the Grain of the Universe: The Church's Witness and Natural Theology* (Grand Rapids, MI: Brazos Press, 2001).

10. Jean Bethke Elshtain, "Christian Contrarian," *Time* (September 17, 2001).

11. Stanley Hauerwas, *A Better Hope: Resources for a Church Confronting Capitalism, Democracy, and Postmodernity* (Grand Rapids, MI: Brazos, 2006), 56. One doesn't have to be a neo-Freudian to recognize here a need to supplant the father figure.

12. Harold Bloom, *The Anxiety of Influence: A Theory of Poetry* (London: Oxford University Press, 1973). Some years ago it dawned on me that the anxiety of influence that lies at the heart of poetic creativity also exists in the Christian theological tradition.

13. John Howard Yoder, *The Politics of Jesus*, 2nd ed. (Grand Rapids, MI: Eerdmans, 1999).

14. *The Politics of Jesus*, 96.

15. For a sample of Hauerwas's language, consider: "I say I'm a pacifist because I am a violent son of a bitch. I'm a Texan. I can feel it in every bone I've got. And I hate the language of pacifism because it's too passive. But by avowing it, I create expectations in others that hopefully will help me live faithfully to what I know is true but that I have no confidence in my own ability to live it at all. That's part of what nonviolence is—the attempt to make our lives vulnerable to others in a way that we need one another. To be against war—which is clearly violent—is a good place to start. But you never know where the violence is in your own life. To say you're nonviolent is not some position of self-righteousness—you kill and I don't. It's rather to make your life available to others in a way that they can help you discover ways you're implicated in violence that you hadn't even noticed," cited in Colman McCarthy, " 'I'm a pacifist because I'm a violent son of a bitch.' A profile of Stanley Hauerwas," *Progressive* (April 2003).

16. *With the Grain of the Universe*, 122.

17. In fact, Hauerwas indicts H. Richard Niebuhr on the same charge of beginning his theological reflection patterned on the world. Stanley Hauerwas, *The Hauerwas Reader*, eds. John Berkman and Michael Cartwright (Durham, NC and London: Duke University Press, 2001), 62–64.

18. In addition to John Milbank, *Theology and Social Theory: Beyond Secular Reason* (Cambridge, MA: B. Blackwell, 1991), see John Milbank et al., *Radical Orthodoxy: A New Theology* (London and New York: Routledge, 1999), and Milbank, "The Poverty of Niebuhrianism" in *The Word Made Strange*.

19. James K. A. Smith, *Introducing Radical Orthodoxy: Mapping a Post-secular Theology* (Grand Rapids, MI: Baker Academic, 2004), 95–100.

20. Gabriel Fackre, "Was Reinhold Niebuhr a Christian?" *First Things* 126 (October 2002): 25–27.

21. Alluding to religion and public life, the late Richard John Neuhaus stated (January 2001) that Niebuhr is "a figure very important to the philosophy of this journal;" the journal's managing editor, Matthew Berke, wrote an appreciative retrospective, "Reinhold Niebuhr *Moral Man and Immoral Society* (1932)" in *First Things* 101 (March 2000): 41–42.

22. See "In Time of War," *First Things* (December 2001): 11–17, and "In a Time of War: An Exchange," *First Things* (February 2002): 11–14.

23. *Just War on Terror: The Burden of American Power in a Violent World* (New York: Basic Books, 2003).

24. See the exchange of views between Stanley Hauerwas and Paul J. Griffiths with a response by Jean Bethke Elshtain, "War, Peace and Jean Bethke Elshtain," *First Things* 136 (October 2003): 41–47.

25. Reinhold Niebuhr (with Angus Dunn), "God Wills Both Justice and Peace," *Christianity and Crisis* 15 (June 13, 1955): 76, cited in Harry R. Davis and Robert C. Good, *Reinhold Niebuhr on Politics* (New York: Charles Scribner's Sons, 1960), 146.

26. As one of his former admirers avers, Stanley Hauerwas engages in hyperbole, often with misleading consequences. See Stephen H. Webb, "The Very American Stanley Hauerwas," *First Things* (June/July 2002). Hauerwas holds, for instance, that Niebuhr in *The Irony of American History* had a love affair with America and that America was, in effect, Niebuhr's church. Hauerwas, *The Hauerwas Reader*, 60, no. 1.

27. Dan Rhodes, "Learning like a Christian: An Interview with Stanley Hauerwas," *Other journal.com*, no. 12 (September 9, 2008).

28. Ted Lewis, ed., *Electing Not to Vote: Christian Reflections on Reasons for Not Voting* (Eugene, OR: Cascade Books, 2008).

29. Reinhold Niebuhr, *Faith and History: A Comparison of Christian and Modern Views of History*, 242.

30. From *Christianity and Crisis*, cited in *Essays in Applied Christianity*, 91–92.

31. Reinhold Niebuhr, *Theology* (February 1940), cited in *Love and Justice*, 49.

32. Friedrich Schleiermacher, *On Religion: Speeches to Its Cultured Despisers*, tr. Richard Crouter (Cambridge: Cambridge University Press, 1996), 21.

33. *Essays in Applied Christianity*, 92.

34. Barack Obama, *The Audacity of Hope* (New York: Crown Publishers, 2006), 218.

35. *Audacity of Hope*, 219; also published in the United Church of Christ source, *United Church News* (August/September 2006), A10–11.

36. For Niebuhr on the theme of empire see Larry L. Rasmussen, "Reinhold Niebuhr," in *Empire and the Christian Tradition: New Readings of Classical Theologians*, eds. Don H. Compier, Kwok Pui-lan, Joerg Rieger (Minneapolis, MN: Augsburg Fortress, 2007), 371–388.

37. *DST*, 4.

38. See Paul Krugman, "For God's Sake," *New York Times*, April 13, 2007.

CHAPTER 7

1. Kegley and Bretall, eds., *Reinhold Niebuhr*, 3.

2. Andrew S. Finstuen, "The Prophet and the Evangelist: The Public 'Conversation' of Reinhold Niebuhr and Billy Graham," *Books and Culture* (July/August 2006) argues that Niebuhr's view of Graham is more complex than is generally understood.

3. Niebuhr came close to a president in power when he was asked to write on "religious freedom" for a pamphlet that celebrated Roosevelt's Four Freedoms. Scott Elledge, *E. B. White: A Biography* (New York: W. W. Norton & Company, 1984), 232–233, tells the story of how in 1942 Archibald MacLeish,

director of the Office of Facts and Figures, enlisted E. B. White to write on freedom of speech and serve as final draftsman of the project with Niebuhr writing on freedom of religion, Max Lerner on freedom from fear, and Malcolm Cowley on freedom from want.

4. As a reader of Niebuhr, President Jimmy Carter is the exception that proves the rule.

5. Frances Perkins, *The Roosevelt I Knew* (New York: Viking, 1946), 148. FDR credited the priest at St. John's Episcopal Church, presumably Howard A. Johnson, with having brought Kierkegaard to his attention.

6. Sonja Lyubomirsky, *The How of Happiness: A New Approach to Getting the Life You Want* (New York: Penguin, 2008).

7. John Brockman, ed., *What Are You Optimistic About? Today's Leading Thinkers on Why Things are Good and Getting Better* (New York: Harper Perennial, 2007), xv.

8. *What Are You Optimistic About?* 27.

9. Undated typescript, Niebuhr Papers, LC, Box 17.

10. *Essays in Applied Christianity*, 40.

11. Rowan Williams, *Why Study the Past? The Quest for the Historical Church* (London: Dartman, Longman and Todd, 2005).

12. *Why Study the Past?* 3.

13. Krister Stendahl, *Paul Among Jews and Gentiles* (Philadelphia, PA: Fortress Press, 1976), 36.

14. "Moral Man and Immoral Society: Rediscovering Reinhold Niebuhr" is online at http://speakingoffaith.publicradio.org/programs/niebuhr-rediscovered/index.shtml.

15. As an interpreter of Black Theology, James H. Cone repeatedly attests to the book's formative power for analyzing racism and other social evils.

16. For a concise overview of Niebuhr in the context of Protestant liberalism see Gary Dorrien, *The Making of American Liberal Theology: Idealism, Realism, and Modernity 1900–1950* (Louisville, KY: Westminster / John Knox Press, 2003), 435–483.

17. Private communication from Perry C. Mason, Professor of Philosophy Emeritus, Carleton College, April 2009.

18. A handwritten letter from his brother, H. Richard Niebuhr, in the 1930s raises questions about Reinhold's "cynicism and skepticism" but ends with Richard describing himself as an "ally if not a soldier in the same division. . .." Niebuhr Papers, LC, Box 9.

19. *Essays in Applied Christianity*, 32.

20. *IAH*, 61–62.

21. From the *New York Times*, November 19, 1928, 22. ProQuest Historical Newspapers, *New York Times* (1851–2001).

22. Norman Cousins, *Anatomy of an Illness as Perceived by the Patient* (New York: W. W. Norton & Company, 1979).

23. Two much-discussed films show humor defying the mechanism of death in the concentration camps: *Life is Beautiful* (1997) starring Roberto Benigni and *Jacob the Liar* (1999) starring Robin Williams.

24. Galen Guengerich, Sermon on "The Irony of American History," All Souls Unitarian Church, New York City, November 2, 2008, http://allsoulsnyc.org/publications/sermons/ggsermons/irony-of-american-history.pdf.

25. See David Brooks, "Man on a Gray Horse," *Atlantic* (September 2002) along with Richard Crouter, "Letter to the Editor," *Atlantic* (November 2002).

26. Erich Fromm, *Beyond the Chain of Illusions*, in a section on Marx and Freud cites John 8:32 along with Terence, "I am a man and nothing human is alien to me."

27. Bill Wylie-Kellermann, "Apologist of Power: The Long Shadow of Reinhold Niebuhr's Christian Realism," *Sojourners* 16, no.3 (March 1987), 14–20.

28. H. Richard Niebuhr in the *Christian Century* (April 6, 1932) reprinted in *War as Crucifixion*, 16.

29. "Intellectual Autobiography," in Kegley and Bretall, eds., *Reinhold Niebuhr*, 3.

30. Friedrich Schleiermacher, *On Religion: Speeches to Its Cultured Despisers*, and Richard Crouter, *Friedrich Schleiermacher: Between Enlightenment and Romanticism* (Cambridge: Cambridge University Press, 2005).

31. Stephen Jay Gould, *Rocks of Ages: Science and Religion in the Fullness of Life* (New York: Ballantine, 1999).

32. *DST*, "Mystery and Meaning," 159.

33. See James Gustafson, *An Examined Faith: The Grace of Self-Doubt* (Minneapolis, MN: Fortress Press, 2004), 106–109, on the faith of Lincoln.

34. "Mystery and Meaning," 162.

35. *Christian Realism and Political Problems*, "Coherence, Incoherence, and the Christian Faith," 197.

36. Terry Eagleton, *Reason, Faith, and Revolution: Reflections on the God Debate* (New Haven, CT: Yale University Press, 2009), 24.

37. Christopher Hitchens, *God Is Not Great: How Religion Poisons Everything* (New York: Twelve / Hachette Book Group USA, 2007), 12.

38. *God Is Not Great*, 282.

39. John Calvin, *Institutes of the Christian Religion*, II.ii.15, tr. Henry Beveridge (Grand Rapids, MI: Eerdmans, 1989), 236.

40. *Reason, Faith, and Revolution: Reflections on the God Debate*, 37.

41. Robinson, "Credo," 23.

42. Niebuhr Papers, LC, Box 17.

43. See epigraph, Chapter 2.

44. Private communication from Edmund Santurri, Professor of Religion, St. Olaf College, March 2009.

45. Michael Gerson, "Obama shows maturity in Nobel speech," *Washington Post*, December 10, 2009; Hendrik Hertzberg, "Presidents and Peace Prizes," *The New Yorker*, December 11, 2009; Andrew Sullivan, "The Tragedy of Hope," *Atlantic Online*, December 11, 2009; Kathleen Parker, "An American triumph at Oslo," *Washington Post*, December 11, 2009; Jon Meacham, "Obama, Faulkner, and the Uses of Tragedy," *Newsweek*, December 12, 2009; Ted Widmer, "Obama's Nobel Speech: Sophisticated and Brave," *New York Times* global edition, December 12, 2009; Jim Wallis, "Obama's Nobel Speech: Reflection and Response," http://blog.sojo.net/2009/12/14/obamas-nobel-speech-reflection-and-response/; E. J. Dionne, "Reality check from Oslo," *Washington Post*, December 14, 2009; David Brooks, "Obama's Christian Realism," *New York Times*, December 15, 2009.

46. Borrowing Timothy Garton Ash's phrase in "A Liberal Translation," *New York Times*, January 25, 2009, Sunday Opinion, 11.

47. Reinhold Niebuhr, "Liberalism: Illusions and Realities," *New Republic* (July 4, 1955), 11–13.

48. "Liberalism: Illusions and Realities," 13.

49. See Arthur Schlesinger, Jr.'s, *The Vital Center: the Politics of Freedom* (Boston, MA: Houghton Mifflin, 1949), the theme of which is echoed in books by Beinart, Mattson, Lieven, and Hulsman.

50. Robin W. Lovin, *Christian Realism and the New Realities* (Cambridge: Cambridge University Press, 2008).

51. Gilkey, *On Niebuhr: A Theological Study*, 20; Robin W. Lovin, "Christian Realism and the Successful Modern State," *Studies in Christian Ethics* 20, no. 1 (2007): 56.

52. *Reflections on the End of an Era*, 4.

53. Kierkegaard (Johannes de Silentio), *Fear and Trembling*, tr. Alastair Hannay (London: Penguin, 1985), 146.

54. Newer work in New Testament studies, Krister Stendahl, *Paul Among Jews and Gentiles* (Philadelphia, PA: Fortress Press, 1976) and John G. Gager, *Reinventing Paul* (Oxford: Oxford University Press, 2000) supports viewing Paul in continuity with his Jewish roots.

55. Niebuhr's prophetism looms large in Andrew J. Bacevich, "Prophets and Poseurs: Niebuhr and our Times"; see also Ronald H. Stone, *Prophetic Realism: Beyond Militarism and Pacifism in an Age of Terror* (New York: T & T Clark, 2005).

INDEX

CPSIA information can be obtained at www.ICGtesting.com
Printed in the USA
BVOW04s1532120314

347438BV00001B/62/P

9 780195 379686